....

LITTLE BOOK
OF
GHOSTS

THE
LITTLE BOOK
OF
GHOSTS

PAUL ADAMS

For Aban, Idris, Isa and Sakina

Cover image: ©iStockphoto.com

First published 2014

The History Press
The Mill, Brimscombe Port
Stroud, Gloucestershire, GL5 2QG
www.thehistorypress.co.uk

British Library Cataloguing in Publication Data.
A catalogue record for this book is available from the British Library.

ISBN 978 0 7509 8563 5

Typesetting and origination by The History Press
Printed in Great Britain by TJ International Ltd, Padstow, Cornwall

CONTENTS

Introduction   7

1.   The Different Categories of Ghost   9
2.   Haunted Houses and Other Buildings   32
3.   Ghosts of Churches, Chapels and Abbeys   53
4.   Haunted Castles and Palaces   60
5.   Ghosts of Stage and Screen   69
6.   Poltergeists and Other Violent Ghosts   75
7.   Haunted Burial Grounds, Woods and Battlefields   92
8.   Haunted Pubs, Taverns and Inns   103
9.   Phantom Animals   112
10. Haunted Objects   126
11. Planes, Trains and Other Haunted Transport   136
12. Ghosts Across the World   157
13. Some Famous Ghost Hunters   168
14. Ghost Societies and Paranormal Organisations   177

Bibliography and Further Reading   183
About the Author   189

INTRODUCTION

This little book is one you might buy for a friend as a present and end up reading yourself. Its subject continues to provoke and fascinate in a technology-obsessed society in which modern science appears to be able to deliver all the answers to questions that, for previous generations, hinted of strange realms beyond the limits of human understanding. Ghosts: who or what are they, why do they appear and where do they come from? This collection contains accounts of many different ghost and supernatural stories drawn from the realms of folklore, ancient and modern history as well as the real-life experiences of ordinary down-to-earth people like you and me. Some can be clearly dismissed as harmless tales; others by their persistence may have some element of the strange or mysterious in them that survives as a grain of truth, but which can be explained away if subjected to a more than superficial glance.

However, some of these ghosts are different. These are the accounts of strange encounters and paranormal experiences that, much to the frustration and chagrin of the hardened sceptic and debunker, refuse to go away, and which provide clear and compelling evidence of a strange haunted realm that interacts and manifests with the material world on a daily basis. They are the experiences that enabled the late writer and researcher Colin Wilson to confidently state that there is as much evidence for ghosts and the paranormal as there is for atoms and electrons.

This growing confidence can be seen in the changing public attitude to reports of ghosts and hauntings. In 1950, a Gallup poll revealed that in post-war Britain only 1 in 10 people said they believed in the paranormal. Fast-forward to the opening decade of the twenty-first century and a similar survey, of 2,060 people, revealed that nearly 4 out of 10 now believe in the existence of ghosts (moreover, these statistics were almost identical with a previous canvas carried out ten years before).

Although public attitudes may be changing, researchers and investigators – the ghost hunters that you will be encountering later on in this book – still cannot say for sure just what ghosts are or why we experience them, for the simple fact is that the evidence is divided. Investigators who are mediums or use mediums to add a psychic dimension to a ghost hunt are more likely to identify apparitions and similar phenomena as being discarnate personalities or the unquiet spirits of the dead. However, there are some researchers who eschew a belief in life after death or a spirit world and propose alternative explanations for the appearance of ghosts and the reasons they walk among us; some of these explanations are included in the pages that follow. Although many of the cases originate from the British Isles, there is a chapter that contains a broad range of international ghosts and you will find a sprinkling of foreign hauntings in several other areas.

Several years ago I read a phrase in the introduction of a similar ghost book which is worth closing with, as it is as relevant today as it was back then. 'The records of organised paranormal investigation show that ghosts appear at all times of the day and night, in many and varied places, and to people from all walks of life, from countesses to cab drivers, and rather than the filmy transparent wraiths of fiction, they can be solid and indistinguishable from real living people. So it is possible that the person sitting next to you on the bus could well be a ghost.' Now there's a thought ...

Paul Adams, 2014

1

THE DIFFERENT
CATEGORIES OF GHOST

Ghosts and ghostly phenomena broadly fall into four basic categories: visual phenomena, normally the sighting of some form of apparition, most often that of a person or human figure; audible phenomena, such as footsteps, voices, music, or other type of recognisable sound; physical phenomena, normally the movement or displacement of objects; and sense phenomena, which can include changes in temperature, smells and odours, together with other forms of experience, such as a feeling of unease, fear or sickness. Hauntings can involve one or more combinations of these basic categories, and the first category, that of apparitions, can itself be divided into several sub-sections which are themselves categories in their own right.

ATMOSPHERIC RECORDINGS OR 'STONE TAPE' GHOSTS

Many reported sightings of ghosts and ghostly figures seem to be little more than brief replays of events from the past that appear to have become imprinted in some unknown way in the fabric or atmosphere of a building or location, and which then become active and replay in the presence of a suitably sensitive or psychically endowed person. As such, they behave like a form of supernatural recording and have no apparent intelligence or awareness of either the witness or their temporary modern surroundings. These stone tape ghosts or residual hauntings go against the idea of a spirit world and the survival of a soul or some part of the human personality after physical death, particularly as they appear along with non-living and inanimate objects such as ghostly vehicles, weapons and other similar items.

The term 'stone tape' was coined by Tom (T.C.) Lethbridge (1901–1971), a former Cambridge don and parapsychologist who has been described as the 'Einstein of the paranormal'. *The Stone Tape* was also the title of a 1972 television play by *Quatermass* writer Nigel Kneale, which dramatised the concept of residual hauntings in a science fiction format.

Stone tape ghosts can involve both small- and large-scale hauntings. In 1968, two Lancashire schoolgirls, Valerie Sandham and Hazel Coulton, both (independently) saw the apparition of a hooded monk-like figure in a classroom at Penwortham Secondary School on the outskirts of Preston. The ghost appeared like a 'moving cardboard cutout, mistily filled in' projected on to the wall and lasted a few minutes before fading away. Over 300 years earlier, on 23 October 1642, Prince Rupert of the Rhine commanded a 15,000-strong army against an equally large opposing force at the Battle of Edgehill in Warwickshire. Over 1,000 men lost their lives in a single afternoon. A month later, shepherds and local people reported seeing visions of soldiers again locked in combat, accompanied by the supernatural sounds of cannon and musket fire. On Christmas Eve of the same year, the Edgehill ghosts returned and a group of investigating officers instructed by Charles II to make enquiries into the happenings confirmed that they had seen the phantom re-enactment for themselves, and had also recognised the apparition of Prince Rupert, the king's nephew, who at the time was still very much alive.

In keeping with their 'playback' nature, apparitions involved in residual hauntings are often seen performing identical tasks or actions every time they make an appearance and are seen by independent witnesses. At Buriton Manor, a Tudor building near Petersfield in Hampshire, the figure of a young maid that haunts the courtyard vanishes through one of the high brick walls where once a doorway existed, leading towards the nearby church. For several years an unidentified figure stepping out of a wall – where a blocked-up doorway was later found during refurbishment work – frightened children in a nursery room at Salisbury Hall near London Colney in Hertfordshire. It is well-known that stone tape apparitions often appear to trace the paths of former building layouts that, in time, have been altered or changed in some way. Ghosts can appear floating above or sunken into the floor or stairway of a house where the level has been either raised or lowered over the years.

A number of stone tape ghosts form cyclical or 'pattern' hauntings, which are said to occur at regular intervals – often on the date of a significant event or anniversary. On 4 June each year, a phantom sailor is said to appear in Ballyheigue Bay, below the ruins of Ballyheigue Castle, on the west coast of Ireland. On 5 July, the anniversary of the Battle of Sedgemoor in 1685, strange lights have been seen over the battlefield and the sounds of fighting men have been heard. Also, every fifty years a ghostly recreation of the three-masted schooner, *Lady Lovibond*, is said to re-enact the moment when, on 13 February 1748, the ship was wrecked on the Goodwin Sands off the coast of Deal in Kent, killing all hands. Several other of these cyclical hauntings are included in later chapters.

Benson Herbert (1912–1991), a ghost hunter active in England during the 1960s and 1970s, felt that all ghostly phenomena could be explained by physics. He described his scientific study of the paranormal 'paraphysics' and set up his own organisation, the Paraphysical Laboratory, in the New Forest near Downton in Wiltshire, in order to carry out his own experiments. Herbert theorised that the massive stone walls of castles and other ancient buildings acted like vast Faraday cages and that the ghosts seen inside them were due to anomalous electrical activity isolated from external radio waves and electromagnetism.

Ghost hunters have come to realise that building work and similar physical interference with the structure and layout of a building can both bring an established haunting to an end and cause a new haunting to take place. During the 1970s, a former dairy in Richmond Road, Kingston-upon-Thames, was used as offices by a practice of chartered surveyors. On several occasions, a cleaner working in the premises after normal hours reported seeing a misty grey apparition, which often appeared behind him and made an attempt to put a hand on his shoulder. After a small kitchen area on the ground floor was converted into a ladies' toilet and the kitchen moved downstairs, the grey man was never seen again. In May 1967, the trade newspaper, the *Whitbread News*, reported on a haunting at The White Horse

public house at Chilham, near Canterbury in Kent. Just over ten years before, builders carrying out alteration work had found an inglenook fireplace hidden behind panelling in one of the rooms. Soon after, the licensees reported seeing the apparition of a tall man with grey hair wearing a black gown, who would appear standing with his back to the inglenook. Several members of staff experienced the ghost, who vanished as soon as he was approached. Interestingly, the phantom man, who some villagers thought might be a seventeenth-century vicar from the church next door, always appeared at exactly 10.10 a.m.

CRISIS GHOSTS

Also known as 'phantasms of the living', crisis ghosts are a type of spontaneous apparition that appear when a person is undergoing some severe personal trauma – such as a life-threatening illness or accident – is close to death or has even passed away. Most often the witness is a close friend or relative, who may not even be aware that the person has died or fallen ill, and who only finds out the true situation at some later time. Crisis ghosts were one of the first areas of psychical phenomena to be studied seriously by researchers in the early years of organised paranormal investigation in the late 1800s.

On 19 March 1917, Mrs Dorothy Spearman was feeding her baby son in her hotel room in Calcutta when she turned and saw her half-brother, Eldred Bowyer-Bower, standing behind her, wearing his full RAF uniform. Thinking that he had been posted to India on leave, she asked him to wait while she put the child to bed. Returning from the crib, Mrs Spearman was surprised to see that the airman was no longer in the room and that her daughter, who had been present, had seen no one. A short time later, it was revealed that Bowyer-Bower had been shot down over the German lines and killed around the same time that he had appeared in the hotel room in Calcutta.

One night in 1941, the novelist Wilbur Wright, returning from leave to RAF Hemswell in Lincolnshire, went to collect some cigarettes from his locker in one of the aircraft hangers. Switching on the light, he found an aircraft gunner, Leading Aircraftman Stoker, rummaging around in his own locker. When Wright asked what he was looking for, Stoker replied: 'I can't find my bloody gloves.' The writer collected his cigarettes and left. The next morning he discovered that the bomber with Stoker on board had been shot down over Dortmund the previous night and all crew, including Stoker, had perished. The mission had taken place at exactly the time that Wright had returned to the base and he subsequently learnt that the gunner had been upset at not being able to find his flying gloves before taking off.

A happier wartime incident of a phantasm of the living was initially published in the Spiritualist newspaper, *Light*. Around 11.30 a.m. on 3 November 1917, Mortimer Noyes, a junior officer in the 1st Battalion, was marching with his platoon to an assembly point in preparation to launch the attack on Passchendaele Ridge. As the column of soldiers continued along the St Julien Road, a lorry approached from the rear and as it began to pass them, Noyes realised that it was his own brother, who was serving in a different regiment, at the wheel. The driver leant out of the window and called out to his brother, 'Cheerio, Den, old lad – best of luck – you'll be alright. God bless you. Can't stop,' after which he accelerated and the lorry moved away up the road and out of sight. Both the company second-in-command and a sergeant who were marching beside Captain Noyes witnessed the incident. Both these men were killed shortly after, but Noyes survived despite being gassed, and in a letter to his brother mentioned the incident a few days before. It transpired that at the time the lorry passed the platoon, Noye's brother had been with his company at Cambrai, over 60 miles away. Both men survived the war and in later years were convinced that the close bond of affection between them had created the strange and moving experience on the St Julien Road that day.

On 1 December 1950, the English composer Ernest John Moeran died from a cerebral haemorrhage while out walking on the pier in the village of Kenmare, County Kerry, in the south of Ireland. A musician friend later reported that an apparition of the composer had appeared to her around the same time that his body had been seen to fall into the water. Although viewed from a distance, the figure was clearly that of Moeran, who acknowledged her before turning and fading from sight.

For many years, one of the most well-known crisis ghost cases was that of Vice-Admiral Sir George Tryon, who was drowned when his flagship HMS *Victoria* collided with another vessel, HMS *Camperdown*, while carrying out naval manoeuvres off Tripoli on 22 June 1893. At the exact moment of the disaster, created by a rogue order from Tryon himself and in which over 300 men lost their lives, a solid and lifelike apparition of the Vice-Admiral wearing his full naval uniform is said to have been seen by a number of guests being entertained by Tryon's wife in their house in fashionable Belgravia in London. The figure, which was not seen by Lady Tryon, walked silently across the room before disappearing; the family received news of the sinking of HMS *Victoria* several hours later. The story was published by folklorist Christina Hole in the early 1940s, but there appears to be little firm evidence that the incident actually took place.

Not all crisis ghosts are those of recently dead or dying people. Some phantasms of the living are just that and appear to be created by strong thoughts or emotions, almost in the manner of a telepathic projection. In the early 1970s, Andrew Green, a ghost hunter and writer, sold a house with a 1-acre plot of land and moved to the village of Iden in East Sussex. Several months later, when the new owner, an engineer and his family, visited Green in his new home, his daughter (who had not met the ghost hunter before) claimed that she had seen his apparition, solid and lifelike, standing and walking in his former garden on a number of occasions. Green, a fanatical gardener, admitted that he missed his old house, particularly the garden and a large rockery he had built himself, and about which he wished to be able to tend again.

In the late 1970s, the American psychical researchers Raymond Bayless and D. Scott Rogo spent two years investigating claims that the spirits of recently deceased persons had made contact with their relations and loved ones using the national telephone system. The results of their enquiry were published in a book, *Phone Calls from the Dead*, in 1979. This brought in further accounts of alleged incidents, one of which took place ten years before and involved a young man named Carl. In 1969, he took a holiday away from his family and rented a room in a cottage owned by an elderly woman known as 'Grandma'. Among several antiques and pieces of *objet d'art* in the room was an old wall-mounted telephone dating from the late nineteenth century, the type which had a separate ear piece and a winding handle to call up the local exchange. After spending a day on the beach, Carl retired to bed and soon fell asleep. At 11.13 p.m., he was woken by the ringing of the old telephone, which he eventually answered. He immediately recognised his father's voice, who told him to make a call to his mother, who had a message for him. When the youth asked for him to bring her to the telephone, his father replied that he was not calling from the house but 'a beautiful place' somewhere else. Then, before Carl could question him further, his father reiterated the need for his son to make the call and rang off. However, when he tried to work the old telephone he found he was unable to get a line and, after several attempts, decided to try again in the morning. The next day, after again trying to work the telephone in his room, Carl spoke with his landlady, who to his amazement told him that that particular device was a curio picked up by her late husband and was not connected to the phone system. When he rang the family home on 'Grandma's' kitchen phone, he spoke directly with his mother, who told him that his father had died the previous evening at exactly the time the old telephone had rung; none of the family knew where Carl was or how to contact him.

INTERACTIVE OR SENTIENT GHOSTS

This category of ghost is similar to the crisis apparition in that the phantom figure appears to show some awareness of the witness and may even speak or attempt some other form of communication. However, by their identity or attire, it is clear that the apparition is that of someone known to be deceased or from a previous era rather than a living person. Interactive ghosts provide some of the best spontaneous evidence (as opposed to information obtained from mediums and psychics) of the possibility of some form of survival or life after death.

A famous Victorian haunting that involved many encounters with a sentient apparition is the Morton case, which took place in Cheltenham, Gloucestershire. In April 1882, the well-to-do Despard family (given the pseudonym Morton in early published accounts) comprising Frederick Despard, a former army captain and his semi-invalid wife Harriet, together with their seven children and several live-in servants, took up residence in a large detached house called 'Denore' in the northern part of the town. On several occasions, the tall figure of a woman in black was seen by both family members – principally nineteen-year-old Rosina Despard who later qualified as a doctor – and a number of the staff, walking in the house and in the garden. The figure, which was solid and lifelike, appeared like a living person and on at least one occasion when addressed, appeared to be on the verge of speaking before moving away. By 1889, the ghost was seldom seen and the haunting appeared to be at an end. However, ghost hunter Andrew MacKenzie was of the opinion that a phantom figure similar to that described by Rosina Despard was still being seen in the neighbourhood as late as the 1980s. The ghost is thought to be that of a widow, Imogen Swinhoe, who lived in the house several years before the arrival of the Despard family and died in September 1878.

An interactive ghost has been seen on at least one occasion at Littlecote Manor in Wiltshire. One afternoon, while walking through the long gallery, a member of staff noticed the figure of a Roundhead soldier sitting in a chair beside one of the windows, who turned his head and watched as the curator approached. The ghost seemed to be fully aware that it was being observed before abruptly fading away. Littlecote had been occupied by Parliamentarian troops during the Civil War.

The film and television actor Telly Savalas (1922–1994), famous for the 1970s police series *Kojak*, claimed to have had a strange and unexplained experience with the eerie apparition of a dead man. One night in the late 1950s, Savalas was returning from a date on Long Island, New York, when his car ran out of petrol. Walking to a nearby service station, he accepted a lift from an effeminate-sounding man wearing a white suit and driving an ordinary-looking Cadillac, who loaned him a dollar to buy some fuel and wrote contact details on a piece of paper so the actor (who had yet to break through into feature films) could return the money. The stranger took him back to the stranded car and, having thanked him, Savalas watched him drive away. The next day, Savalas rang the telephone number he'd been given and spoke with the man's wife, who initially thought the actor was playing a joke: her husband had been dead for two years. Soon after, the two met in New York. The widow confirmed that the suit Savalas had seen the stranger wearing was the one he had been buried in. The effeminate voice may have been due to the fact that her husband, who normally spoke in a deep tone, had committed suicide by shooting himself through the neck.

TIMESLIP GHOSTS

This category of haunting or paranormal experience involves not only the appearance of phantom forms or apparitions, but also some shift or change in the localised environment which itself becomes part of the supernormal experience. Witnesses to such events claim to have seen a building or location as it would have appeared at some point in the past, or even as it eventually appears at some future time. Although relatively uncommon, there are a number of specific and interesting cases.

The most well-known timeslip haunting, known as the Versailles Visions, has divided the opinions of researchers since details were first published over 100 years ago. On a hot summer day in August 1901, while visiting the gardens of the Petit Trianon, two former principals of St Hugh's College, Oxford – Miss Moberly and Miss Jourdain – seemingly slipped back in time and walked through the grounds as they would have been during the reign of King Louis XIV. The two women claimed to have seen buildings and garden features that were no longer in existence and encountered solid-looking apparitions of courtiers in authentic period clothing as well as the ghost of Marie Antoinette herself. They published an account of their experiences together with details of later visits to Versailles and accounts of historical research into the palace and its gardens in a book, *An Adventure*, which appeared in 1911 and became something of a supernatural bestseller. In 1965, it was suggested that the poet Robert de Montesquiou, a regular visitor to Versailles around the turn of the century, often spent time there together with his friends dressed in period costume and that the two women had in fact simply witnessed the outdoor rehearsal for a *tableau-vivant* in full costume. However, there are several reports of other sightings of apparitions in and around the grounds of the Petit Trianon since Miss Moberly and Miss Jourdain had their adventure and as such, the case is not so easy to dismiss.

In the early hours of 4 August 1951, two Englishwomen, Dorothy Norton and her sister-in-law Agnes Norton (both pseudonyms), who were holidaying at Puys near Dieppe in northern France were awakened by a series of protracted and unusual noises. What at first seemed to be a breaking storm developed into the unmistakable sound of a military conflict that appeared to be taking place in the immediate vicinity: the women heard the drone of dive-bombing aircraft, accompanied by explosions and the rattle of gunfire, together with the shouts and cries of fighting soldiers. The 'battle' began around 4.20 a.m. and continued in varying levels of intensity until just before 7.00 a.m., after which all became quiet. The Nortons' experience appeared to be an aural timeslip haunting, in which the two women were able to experience a real-time soundtrack of the disastrous Dieppe Raid which took place in the same area on 19 August 1942, the details of which were unfamiliar to them, although both knew that a battle had been fought there during the Second World War. The case was subsequently investigated by two members of the Society for Psychical Research and despite alternative explanations being put forward, in particular the sound of a dredging ship being mistaken for battle noises, it remains convincing.

One midsummer's day in 1954, London booksellers Eric and Irina Barton travelled by train to Dorking in Surrey for a walk on the slopes of the North Downs. Extending their walk to the village of Wotton, the Bartons visited the parish church of St John and spent some time examining the tomb of seventeenth-century diarist John Evelyn. Afterwards, the couple left the churchyard and followed an overgrown single-track pathway up the hill, where they eventually sat to eat their lunch on a wooden bench. Now feeling cold and uncharacteristically depressed, the two walkers suddenly became aware of an intense silence which was broken only by the sound of a barking dog and a woodsman's axe, which seemed to come from a spot further down the valley. Suddenly, Irina noticed three men, all dressed in black and wearing hats – one of whom looked unmistakably like a clergyman – standing a short distance behind them. Frightened by their sudden appearance, the couple moved on and eventually made their way back to Dorking railway station. The following week, Eric Barton decided to return to the area and made some startling discoveries: the overgrown path near the church, the bench seat and even the wooded hillside through which they had walked did not exist; the area was completely different, even down to a single-track railway that they remembered crossing which, at the time of their experience, consisted of two railway lines. The mysterious Wotton timeslip has never been explained.

Not all timeslip hauntings involve human activity; in the 1940s, the Society for Psychical Research published a report about a phantom landscape. In March 1938, a man named Bates was walking along the cliff path above Mansands Cove between Churston Ferrers and Dartmouth in Devon. As he looked ahead, he saw an open panorama of fields, across which the footpath he was following crossed and disappeared into the distance. As he climbed up on to a stile and made to jump down the other side, the landscape in front suddenly vanished and he found he was seconds away from falling over the cliff edge down on to the beach below; the entire landscape had in fact been a ghostly mirage.

The famous Swiss psychiatrist Carl Jung (1875–1961) also claimed to have had a mysterious timeslip experience. In the early 1930s, accompanied by a friend, he visited the tomb of Galla Placidia, the daughter of Roman Emperor Theodosius I, in Ravenna, Italy. The two men spent some time examining a series of exquisite mosaics inside the mausoleum, which appeared to be illuminated by a curious pale blue luminescence. Afterwards, Jung and his companion tried to buy postcards of the mosaics but were unable to find any of the ones they had seen. Later back in Zurich, Jung asked a friend who was visiting Ravenna to take some photographs of the murals but he was also unsuccessful: the mosaics that the psychiatrist described seeing did not in fact exist, having been destroyed by a fire several hundred years before.

POLTERGEISTS

Fear of the unknown makes the subject of ghosts and hauntings a taboo one for many people, but perhaps the most frightening of all supernatural phenomena, even for ghost hunters and believers in the paranormal, is that associated with the poltergeist. Characterised by the often violent movement and destruction of objects, poltergeist activity has been recorded over the course of several hundred years but despite being well documented in modern times, ghost hunters and psychical researchers still cannot decide exactly what causes a poltergeist haunting to take place.

Poltergeist is a German word variously translated as 'noise spirit', 'noisy ghost' or 'knocking ghost'. Unlike traditional hauntings, which are essentially restricted to a particular location or environment, most often a haunted house or building, poltergeists are person-focused hauntings which take place around and in the presence of a particular family member (described as the 'nexus' of the haunting), most often an adolescent youth or teenager. However, some poltergeist cases have been reported where an adolescent focus has been absent and there are cases of traditional hauntings that also contain episodes of poltergeist-like activity.

One of the earliest cases to display poltergeist-type phenomena occurred in Ravenna, Italy in AD 530. The first British case of which a detailed account survives took place in North Aston in Oxfordshire in 1591 when, according to reports, stones were thrown around and seen to fall from the ceiling of a farmhouse belonging to a Mr George Lee and his family.

A famous poltergeist case, known as the Drummer of Tedworth, took place in a house in Wiltshire in 1661 and lasted for over two years. The home of John Mompesson was plagued by a wealth of strange and frightening phenomena including the movement of objects, loud drumming sounds, mysterious voices, unexplained lights, claw marks, animal noises, and many unpleasant smells. Children in the house reported seeing apparitions and were themselves levitated out of their beds, while a manservant claimed to have awoken to find a dark figure with glowing red eyes standing at the foot of his bed. The English writer Joseph Glanvill (1636–1680) visited the house and reported strange sounds and noises, which he included in his *Saducismus Triumphatus*, published in 1661. The happenings appeared to be centred on an itinerant drummer, a demobbed Roundhead soldier, who was arrested and jailed for nuisance after residents of the nearby town of Ludgarshall complained of his incessant noise. The drummer, who served a period in Gloucester Gaol for theft before being banished from the area, claimed he had sent the ghosts to plague the household as revenge on John Mompesson who himself had taken exception to the annoying drumbeating and to whose house the confiscated drum had been taken.

In the past, the phenomena associated with poltergeist activity have been interpreted as the work of possessing demons and evil spirits. The screenplay of director William Friedkin's groundbreaking 1973 horror film *The Exorcist*, taken from the novel of the same name by William Peter Blatty, was based on real events. The Cottage City Poltergeist case took place in Prince George's County, Maryland, US, in 1949 and involved a thirteen-year-old schoolboy variously known as Roland Doe, Rob Doe and Robbie Mannheim. In early January, knocks, scratching sounds and other noises including unusual footsteps began disturbing the home of a small family in Cottage City. Household items began moving by themselves, and soon it became apparent that Roland was the focus of the mysterious and increasingly frightening activity. Scratch marks appeared on his skin, his bed vibrated as he lay on the mattress and on several occasions the teenager had the covers pulled off his body as if by unseen hands and was physically thrown on to the floor. A Lutheran minister, Revd Miles Schulze, summoned by the boy's parents, spent time in the house and witnessed a number of strange incidents, including on one occasion a chair – with Roland seated on it with his legs raised off the floor – sliding by itself across the bedroom. After undergoing medical tests, Roland was eventually examined by a group of Jesuit priests at the Georgetown University Hospital in Washington DC, who claimed the youth was possessed by an evil spirit and, over the course of several weeks, performed a protracted exorcism. In April 1949, Roland appeared to recover and the mysterious phenomena never returned. By the time Joseph Banks Rhine and his wife Louisa, noted researchers from the Parapsychology Department at Duke University in North Carolina, became interested in the case, the Cottage City Poltergeist had departed.

ELECTRONIC VOICE PHENOMENA (EVP)

Allegedly supernormal sounds captured on recording equipment during the course of vigils and investigations in haunted houses and other locations, Electronic Voice Phenomena or EVPs are cited by many ghost hunters and paranormal researchers as evidence of the involvement of discarnate spirits and entities in hauntings and similar psychic activity. Most EVPs take the form of individual words or short staccato sentences, which are audible on analogue or digital tape recorders, either appearing spontaneously or in response to specific questions posed by team members during the course of an investigation. The first person to encourage the serious study of EVPs was the Swedish psychologist, Konstantin Raudive (1909–1974) whose pioneering book *Breakthrough* was published in an English translation by Peter Bander, who also wrote on the subject in 1971. Encouraged by Raudive's work, other Western researchers began carrying out their own experiments. They included in England, Raymond Cass (1921–2002), George Bonner (1924–1997) and Judith Chisholm; in America, George Meek (1910–1999) and Sarah Estep (d. 2008); while the Swedish film producer Friedrich Jürgenson produced many EVP recordings before his death in 1987. Sceptics argue that the EVPs are simply created by a combination of ordinary static and the ability of the human brain to create seemingly intelligible words out of random sounds, with the result that like 'orbs' and similar visual anomalies on photographs and video recordings, EVPs remain a controversial part of modern paranormal investigation.

MAN-MADE OR ARTIFICIAL GHOSTS

Although many ghosts occur spontaneously and the reasons for their haunting are at present unknown, there are a number of instances where genuine paranormal phenomena including the sighting of apparitions has been created on purpose by researchers and other interested people as part of specific experiments into the supernatural. A number of spiritualist mediums, both past and present, have claimed to be able to materialise the spirits of the departed as solid figures during the course of séances and similar psychic meetings. These 'ghosts in solid form' can also be considered to fall into the category of man-made or artificial ghosts.

Like many mediums of the early twentieth century, the Frenchwoman Marthe Béraud (1886–*c*. 1943), also known as Eva Carrière or Eva C, claimed to be able to create solid spirit forms within the closed environment of the séance room. In 1905, she was investigated by the eminent physiologist Charles Richet, who was convinced of her genuineness and championed her mediumship in his book *Thirty Years of Psychical Research*, published in 1922. However, not long after Richet visited Marthe in Algiers, a coachman who worked at the Villa Carmen where the sittings took place claimed that the séances had been faked and that he had, by dressing up in a helmet and a white sheet, impersonated the ghost of a 300-year-old Brahman Hindu called Bien Boa that Richet had both examined and photographed. In the 1920s, Marthe, now calling herself Eva C, was again investigated by researchers from both England and Germany but her phenomena was again found to be fraudulent. Several incriminating photographs taken during her séances showed that the spirit faces seen by observers were in fact cut out of French newspaper *Le Miroir*. Little is known of Marthe following these investigations and it appears likely that she died in occupied France sometime in the early 1940s.

In the mid-1970s, Frank Smyth, the editor of the occult and paranormal journal *Man, Myth and Magic*, decided to invent a ghost story to fill up a blank page in his magazine; the publication deadline was looming and he was short on copy for that particular issue. He created the story of the Phantom Vicar of Ratcliffe Wharf, a murderous cleric from the 1600s who robbed the sailors from merchant ships in their lodgings and for good measure beat them over the head with a club as they lay sleeping, later disposing of their bodies in the Thames. Smyth wrote up the piece and included several spurious witness sightings of the sinister ghost, but even before the story was published he met a dockworker who claimed that the ghost was actually real and that his grandfather had told him fireside stories about it. After the article appeared, other writers included the case in their books, unaware that it was a hoax, and soon several people had claimed to have seen the ghostly vicar in the Wapping area of East London. An episode of the BBC series *Leap in the Dark* also featured the story, and included an experiment organised by Colin Wilson in which Jean Morgan, a hypnotised subject, was made to see the ghost during a visit to Wapping accompanied by a film crew.

In 1972, the Canadian parapsychologists George and Iris Owen, along with several other members of the Toronto Society for Psychical Research, decided to carry out an experiment to see if it was possible to create a real ghost. They invented an imaginary character, Sir Philip Aylesford, a Royalist secret agent in the time of Charles II, who supposedly committed suicide in 1654 at the age of thirty after a doomed love affair with a gypsy woman. The group met at the Owens' house and tried to make contact with the imaginary Philip by table-tilting. After several unsuccessful sessions, knocks and raps were heard and the table began moving beneath their hands. The researchers established a knocking code and began communicating with 'Philip' himself. During the three years that the experiment was held, the group also reported other happenings, including the movement of chairs and other furniture. The Toronto group felt that there were no spirits involved in the ghostly happenings: the poltergeist effects (termed macro-PK or macro-psychokinesis) were created by the sitters' subconscious minds. Since then, other experimental ghosts have been created by similar groups including 'Lilith', a spy from the Second World War; 'Sebastian', a medieval alchemist from Quebec; and 'Axel', a mysterious ghost from the future.

Between 1993 and 1998, a protracted series of psychic sittings, now known under the collective title of the Scole Experiment, took place in the cellar of an isolated farmhouse near Diss in Norfolk. Led by paranormal investigator Robin Foy, a group of mediums and spiritualists attempted to bring traditional physical mediumship into the modern age. Through a 'spirit team' of discarnate personalities, the group claimed to have experienced a vast array of paranormal phenomena including materialisations, spirit lights and physical apports, as well as psychic images imprinted on unused camera film. Several members of the Society for Psychical Research, including Professor David Fontana and Montague Keen, attended several of the Scole sessions and were favourably impressed. The group claimed to be working with a different type of spirit-world technology that did not rely on both traditional 'ectoplasm' and the presence of a developed physical medium, and that with time for development, other groups would be able to produce similar phenomena.

THE FACELESS GHOSTS

One common theme present across many reported experiences by witnesses of ghostly figures and apparitions is the lack of features or absence of a face. While the actual figure of the ghost or its clothes can be described in quite remarkable detail, the face often appears in many cases to be either obscured in some way, hidden by clothing or, in a number of cases, frighteningly absent. It would appear that whatever forces, be they spiritual or supernormal, that come together to create the apparitional experience often have trouble in forming a representation of the face or features, the most individual and expressive part of the human form. This could explain why many traditional stories and legends feature reports of headless ghosts and apparitions.

In 1985, Sharon Grenny, a council tenant, was forced to flee with her young family from their house in Sutcliffe Avenue, Grimsby, after several encounters with a faceless monk-like apparition that she described as having a wide hood that was drawn up obscuring its features.

In the late 1970s, a local Catholic priest, Father Don Breen, carried out an exorcism in a council flat in the Green Court tower block in Hockwell Ring, Luton, after the tenant, Jennifer Davies, reported several incidences of poltergeist activity and the appearance of a tall monk-like figure whose face appeared to be heavily burnt and almost missing.

A frightening apparition of a faceless woman is traditionally said to haunt marshland on the east coast of England at dusk. The figure, described as wearing a bonnet that is completely empty and in which no head or face can be seen, is accompanied by a roaring wind that sweeps people aside as she passes by.

Chicksands Priory, near Shefford in Bedfordshire, is traditionally haunted by the ghost of a disgraced nun, Bertha Rosata, who has been seen on a number of occasions over the years. In 2008, she was reported as appearing as a solid but faceless figure by a visiting medium, Margaret Rolph, who described the features as similar to a television screen with the picture tuned out.

The former Battlefield House (now demolished), at one time a private home and later a tailor's shop in Chequer Street, St Albans, was haunted by the sounds of chanting monks and ghostly fighting men – possibly a psychic imprint of the First Battle of St Albans which took place close by in 1455 – as well as the apparition of a faceless man wearing a beaver hat.

A tall, faceless figure dressed in green and surrounded by a strange grey mist haunts the Four Ashes Road between Cryers Hill and Terriers, 2 miles north of High Wycombe in Buckinghamshire. It was seen one night in 1978 by Phil Mullett, a twenty-eight-year-old warehouseman, and again on

20 September 1986 by a young couple driving along the road just before midnight. All the witnesses described seeing a tall figure around 2m in height, greenish in colour but without any visible face or hands.

SHADOW PEOPLE AND NON-HUMAN HAUNTINGS

A relatively recent category of ghostly phenomena now accepted by some paranormal researchers involves the appearance of 'shadow people', dark ephemeral apparitions variously interpreted as inter-dimensional beings, malevolent spirits or similar entity-like creatures. Although traditional hauntings do on occasion involve encounters with shadowy and insubstantial figures, this category elevates the phenomenon to a distinct level and credits the apparition or ghost with sentient abilities, particularly some form of distinct awareness, intelligence and purpose. They are most often reported watching over people as they lie in bed, as well as emerging from cupboards and walking out of solid walls. Some reports allege physical attacks and violence and they are also associated with UFO phenomena, including alien abductions and extraterrestrial life forms.

The American writer Heidi Hollis is credited as being the originator of the 'shadow people' phenomenon in the early 2000s, since when other researchers have considered them a worthwhile area of study. In 2005, American author Rosemary Ellen Guiley began an ongoing project to collect a database of 'shadow people' encounters and experiences.

Some writers associate 'shadow people' with djinn (or jinn), another category of non-human ghost perhaps better described as primordial spirits or 'elementals'. The earliest written accounts of djinn are between 4,000 and 6,000 years old and originate in ancient Arabia, Sumeria, Persia, Assyria and Babylonia. Djinn are most associated with the religion of Islam, where the Qur'an describes them as invisible beings created from 'smokeless flame' which, along with angels, inhabit the earth with mankind, and are a convenient explanation for most types of paranormal phenomena including ghosts and apparitions, poltergeists, haunted houses and diabolical human possession. A growing trend among some researchers is to interpret hauntings, specifically poltergeist hauntings and similar phenomena, as evidence of the existence of djinn in the modern world.

2

HAUNTED HOUSES AND
OTHER BUILDINGS

The earliest record of the investigation of a haunted house is contained in a series of letters by the Roman orator Pliny the Younger in the first century AD. Pliny describes a villa in Athens that was haunted by the apparition of a grey-haired old man fettered in chains. Several occupants had moved out because of the disturbance and the owner found it difficult to find tenants who would stay for any length of time. A philosopher, attracted by the local tales as well as the disarmingly low rent, moved in and observed the appearance of the ghost, which disappeared at a particular spot in the corner of the courtyard. When this was excavated, in the presence of the philosopher (accompanied by a local magistrate), the skeleton of a man bound in chains and which had lain undisturbed for many years was discovered. After the skeleton was given a proper burial, the sinister apparition was never seen again.

The stately homes of England are home to a rich variety of ghosts and hauntings. Sawston Hall, a Tudor mansion on the outskirts of Cambridge, has all the ingredients of a classic haunted house. In 1553, John Huddleston gave shelter to Mary Tudor ('Bloody Mary'), who was being pursued by armed soldiers under the command of the Duke of Northumberland. Mary escaped on horseback disguised as a dairymaid and the original house was destroyed by fire. After her ascent to the throne and marriage to Philip of Spain, John Huddleston was knighted and Sawston Hall was rebuilt. There are several reported ghosts here: a Grey Lady haunts the Tapestry Room and the sound of a spinet has also been heard; Mary Tudor herself is said to walk in the grounds, while at the beginning of the nineteenth century, a poltergeist is said to have ripped off the clothes of the wife of the village tanner, leaving her 'ashamed, shocked and speechless with terror'.

The Brown Lady of Raynham Hall in Norfolk has become one of England's best-known ghosts, thanks to an extraordinary incident that took place on 19 September 1936. Captain Hubert Provand, a *Country Life* photographer accompanied by an assistant, Indre Shira, on an assignment to take pictures of the interior of the

seventeenth-century house for a forthcoming article, were setting up their equipment at the foot of the main staircase when Shira called out that he could see a shadowy figure moving down the steps towards them. Provand quickly uncapped the camera lens while his assistant fired off the flashgun, at which point the ghostly figure vanished. When the plate was developed, what has become an iconic 'ghost' photograph was revealed. The phantom is said to be that of Lady Dorothy Walpole, sister of Prime Minister Robert Walpole, who died at Raynham Hall from smallpox in 1726. A famous sighting took place in 1836 when Captain Frederick Marryat, a friend of novelist Charles Dickens, fired a pistol at her apparition, clad in a brown brocade dress, as it glided down one of the upper corridors. The Brown Lady was first seen at Christmas 1835 and it was reported that she had made an appearance ten years before her portrait was taken by Provand and Shira in 1936.

Ham House, situated on the Thames, south of Richmond in Surrey, was built in 1610 by Sir Thomas Vavasour, Knight Marshal to James I. It is haunted by Elizabeth Murray, Duchess of Lauderdale, who died here on 5 June 1698 at the age of seventy-two. The apparitions of both the duchess and her pet dog have been seen inside the house: ghostly footprints were found impressed into new floor polish on the main staircase following a Ghost Club investigation in November 2003, while in June 2009, Colin Iles, a visitor from Croydon, claimed to have photographed the duchess' ghost during a visit to the house with his girlfriend.

The apparition of a disembodied arm at one time haunted Capesthorne Hall, near Macclesfield in Chesire, built in the early 1700s and home to the Bromley-Devenport family. One night in 1958, the son of the then owner, Sir William Bromley-Devenport, awoke to see a hand and naked forearm 'groping towards the window near his bed'. By the time the young man had recovered from the shock, the arm had disappeared.

The heavy footsteps that haunt Chenies Manor House near Amersham in Buckinghamshire are thought to be those of Charles I, who spent time here under house arrest by Cromwell's soldiers.

Like many historic houses, the Elizabethan Levans Hall in Cumbria, built in 1580 by James Bellingham on the site of a former fortified tower, boasts several ghosts. Its most famous apparition is the Grey Lady, thought to be an old gypsy woman who starved to death after being turned away at the door many years ago. Her ghost has been seen on a number of occasions, from the time that horse-drawn coaches delivered visitors to the hall up until modern times. She appears as a realistic female form which materialises suddenly in the vehicle's path and then just as quickly vanishes from sight. A small black phantom dog has also been seen running outside, while another female ghost, the Pink Lady, only appears in the presence of children.

A ghostly priest haunts Smithills Hall near Halliwell in Greater Manchester. The Protestant martyr, George Marsh, a former farmer, was held here shortly before his trial and execution at Boughton on 24 April 1554. It is his apparition that has been seen passing through the Green Room, while a footprint, preserved in the stone floor and allegedly made by Marsh stamping his foot in frustration at the injustice of his fate, is said to bleed once a year on the anniversary of his death.

THE ENFIELD POLTERGEIST

One of the most widely publicised cases of modern haunting took place not in a stately home or mist-shrouded castle, but in a small council house in the North London suburb of Enfield in 1977. The Enfield Poltergeist, as it is now internationally known, quickly made newspaper headlines as photographs of violent phenomena and levitating children fuelled a controversy which still provokes reactions over thirty-five years after the event. On the evening of 30 August 1977, knocks and banging sounds were heard by

Mrs Peggy Hodgson as she prepared to put her four children to bed. Thirteen-year-old Rose, Peter, aged ten, eleven-year old Janet and her seven-year-old brother Jimmy all heard the noises and watched as pieces of household furniture – including an easy chair and a beside cabinet – began moving about by themselves. The poltergeist activity quickly escalated, transforming the house in Green Street, Enfield, into a paranormal bedlam: objects flew through the air, doors slammed by themselves and the children were pulled out of their beds, as if by unseen hands. The local police and soon after a reporter and photographer from the *Daily Mirror* visited the house and all witnessed the phenomena. The focus of the haunting appeared to be young Janet Hodgson, who was caught on a remotely operated camera seemingly flying through the air and was also recorded speaking in a strange guttural voice which identified itself as Bill Wilkins, a former occupant who had died in the house several years before.

The case divided the London-based Society for Psychical Research, several members of which visited Enfield while the poltergeist was active. Senior members John Beloff and Anita Gregory, who spent time in the house later on in the investigation, were unimpressed and felt that the Hodgson children were faking most if not all of the phenomena in order to gain attention. However, two other researchers, Maurice Grosse and Guy Lyon Playfair, both of whom were involved almost from the outset, were convinced that much of the happenings at Green Street were genuine. As well as the physical movement of objects, they reported several spontaneous fires, the appearance of apparitions (one of whom was said to be that of Maurice Grosse himself, seen through a frosted glass door panel by a visitor), and perhaps the most bizarre happening of all, the alleged teleportation of Janet Hodgson through the party wall into the house next door.

After over a year of almost continual disturbance, the haunting finally ceased in October 1978, coinciding with (and possibly even brought about by) a visit to Enfield by Dono Gmelig-

Meyling, a psychic medium from Holland brought over to England by a Dutch journalist, who claimed to be able to bring peace to the Hodgsons' home. Apart from a brief resurgence of a very mild nature lasting only a few days in April 1979, this proved to be true.

💀 💀 💀

Not all hauntings involve the appearance of phantom figures. One of the most well-known supernatural stories from the border between England and Scotland involves Dilston Hall, also known as Dilston Castle, overlooking the Devil's Water brook, 3 miles east of Hexham. Here a ghostly light, glimpsed in the empty windows of the ruined tower, is thought to be the phantom of Lady Derwentwater whose husband, Sir James Radcliffe, was executed in London for his part in the 1715 Jacobite rebellion. Sir James is also said to return to his former home: he is the headless figure seen wandering at dusk through the grounds.

THE ROMANS IN THE CELLAR

One of the most convincing and well-known accounts of the sighting of ghostly figures took place in the city of York in 1953. Harry Martindale, an eighteen-year-old apprentice plumber, was carrying out work alone in the cellar of the historic Treasurer's House close to York Minster when he heard the sound of what appeared to be a horn call coming from close by. Looking up, Martindale saw a column of around twenty Roman soldiers, which materialised out of a brick wall close to where he was working on a ladder and walked in procession across the width of the cellar area before vanishing into the wall opposite. The vision lasted nearly half a minute and the ghostly figures were only visible from knee-level upwards. Martindale described the soldiers as appearing tired and dispirited in appearance. Twenty years later, in the early 1970s, archaeological excavations in the same cellar area uncovered the Via Decumana, the original Roman road that the spectral soldiers had been walking along in the youth's incredible paranormal vision.

🐾 🐾 🐾

As well as ghostly figures, houses can be haunted by strange and unpleasant atmospheres linked to tragic events from the past. In 1935, John Wells, a Middlesex County Council employee, and his wife rented rooms in a house in Greenford, West London, which the couple had seen advertised in a local shop window. Viewing the house for the first time, Mr Wells asked to use the lavatory and while he was in the bathroom, he became overwhelmed by a feeling of immense fear bordering on blind terror, which vanished as soon as he left the room. During the two years that the couple lived at the house, both were aware of the atmosphere the bathroom generated, during the day as well as at night, but it was some time before they eventually admitted it to each other. The Wells were not the only people who were disturbed by the vibes inside the innocent-looking bathroom: a worker from Ireland who lived with them for some time described the atmosphere as 'evil'. Eventually, John Wells got to the bottom of the mystery after meeting a man who had known the house's previous owner. He had had nothing but bad luck during the time he had owned the property and had eventually died in an accident. The bathroom's evil atmosphere stemmed from an incident that took place during the house's construction, when one of the builders who had debt problems hanged himself from the lavatory cistern.

BORLEY RECTORY AND ITS GHOSTS

The Revd Henry Dawson Ellis Bull built the famous 'most haunted house in England' in the small village of Borley on the Essex/Suffolk border in 1862–3. He was the head of a wealthy local landowning family with a long history in the area who, like his father, had been born in nearby Pentlow. Henry and Caroline Bull themselves had a large family of at least thirteen children and the rectory, later extended in 1877, developed into a rambling red-brick building set in expansive grounds opposite the twelfth-century church. Henry Bull died in 1892 and was succeeded by his son Harry, who held the living until his own death in 1927. During the years of the Bulls at Borley, the rectory gained a reputation for being a haunted house and several members of the family claimed to have seen ghosts and phantom figures. They included the form of a woman in white, a ghostly coach and horses, the apparition of a dark clothed man wearing a tall hat, and most famously, the ghost of a nun which haunted the roadway and the garden. On 28 July 1900, the apparition was seen by four of the Bull sisters on the lawn in daylight and a local tradition held that one of the rectory's windows was bricked up to prevent the unhappy-looking figure from peering in on the family at mealtimes.

Following the Revd Harry Bull's death, the remaining family members moved to another house, Chilton Lodge in nearby Great Cornard, and Borley Rectory stood empty for several months. In October 1928, the Revd Guy Eric Smith and his wife Mabel took up the living and together with their maid, Mary Pearson, moved into the large lonely building. The Smiths were at Borley for less than two years and, during their time there, brought the haunting to national attention. The couple described hearing footsteps and seeing a strange light in the window of an unoccupied room; they reported the servant bells ringing by themselves and Mary Pearson claimed to have seen the phantom coach crossing the lawn and also encountering the apparition of a headless man. A reporter from the *Daily Mirror*, along with ghost hunter Harry Price (*see* Chapter 13), visited Borley. A séance was held in the Blue Room, a first-floor bedroom that was allegedly the most haunted spot in the house, and incidents of a poltergeist nature took place.

For five years beginning in October 1930, the Revd Lionel Foyster, a cousin of the Bulls, lived at Borley with his young wife Marianne and their adopted daughter, Adelaide. During their stay, the Foysters also reported many strange and inexplicable incidents of a ghostly nature, including stone throwing and the violent movement of objects; Marianne Foyster claimed to have seen the ghost of Harry Bull and the Revd Foyster compiled a diary of the activities of the Borley ghosts that he called 'the goblins'. In 1932, a spiritualist circle from nearby Marks Tey visited the house and carried out an exorcism, after which the phenomena appeared to die down and the Foysters eventually left Borley in October 1935. The rectory itself remained empty as the next incumbent, Alfred Henning, elected to live nearby in the neighbouring parish of Liston, to which Borley had by now been joined. Henning became interested in the rectory haunting, however, and in May 1937 allowed Harry Price to rent the building in order to carry out a year-long ghost hunt. Price recruited a group of observers using an advertisement in *The Times* newspaper and prepared an instruction book on how to carry out the investigation. Several of his observers reported incidents of phenomena, including the movement of objects and ghostly footsteps, and Price later wrote about Borley and the investigation in his book, *The Most Haunted House in England*, which was published in 1940, and another, later volume, entitled *The End of Borley Rectory* (1946). By this time, the rectory itself had been destroyed by fire and the ruins demolished.

In 1956, the Society for Psychical Research published a critical report that dismissed much of the evidence for haunting at Borley and accused Harry Price (who died in 1948) of faking phenomena in order to gain publicity from the case. Since then several more books have been published, including *The Ghosts of Borley* (1973), *The Enigma of Borley Rectory* (1996) and *The Borley Rectory Companion* (2009), and the case continues to be both popular and controversial. Today nothing remains of the famous haunted rectory but ghost hunters still visit the area in the hope of collecting evidence of continued haunting on the site and in the nearby church.

☠ ☠ ☠

Ghosts and other paranormal phenomena alleged to have been seen and experienced in and around Borley Rectory over the course of many years include: a phantom nun or nun-like figure; a man in dark clothes (sometimes described as a monk to fit in with a local legend); a screaming girl; a woman in a white dress; the apparition of a former rector; a small black man or imp; the ghost of a former gardener; a man in a bowler hat and another in a cloak (seen during the night of the disastrous fire in 1939); a phantom coach; a phantom cat and a strange insect; a haunted coat; mysterious wall writing; crashing noises; the appearance, disappearance and movement of objects; stone-throwing; bell-ringing; footsteps; a strange light; mysterious smells and odours; psychic touches; a 'cold spot'; voices; spontaneous fires and – in Borley church – the sound of ghostly organ music.

OTHER 'MOST HAUNTED' HOUSES

During the 1970s, Sandford Orcas Manor House near Sherborne in Dorset gained a reputation as one of the most haunted buildings in the country. The then tenants, Colonel Francis Claridge and his wife, claimed that the house had been cursed by a Saxon lord and was haunted by over twenty ghosts including three child poltergeists, a spectral dog, a white-haired old lady in a red silk dress, a screaming lunatic, the sound of a spinet, a procession of hooded monks, a woman in black, a 7ft-tall Georgian rapist, and the apparition of a farmer wearing a white smock. Claridge, who died in 1986, claimed he had woken one night to find the figure of a priest standing over the bed in the act of trying to smother the couple with his habit: the ghost was that of a cleric who had murdered a man in the same room many years before. The gardens were also haunted by several phantoms, including an Elizabethan woman and a ghostly gypsy. Following the departure of the Claridges, the owner, Sir Christopher Medlycott, played down the haunting, claiming that his former tenants had made up 'a ghost a day', with the result that this strange and fascinating house appears to have now lost its 'most haunted' crown.

The Catholic martyr John Wall, executed in 1679, is said to be one of the many ghosts that haunt Chingle Hall, a thirteenth-century manor house at Goosnargh near Preston in Lancashire. Several former owners have seen monk-like figures walking in the house and in the garden, while in the Priest Room, said to be the most haunted part of the house, the apparition of a man with shoulder-length hair has been seen, as well as a disembodied hand and a figure wearing whitish robes. Ghost hunters in the early 1980s reported knocking noises and the sound of heavy footsteps has been picked up by a tape recorder.

Ballechin House, the 'most haunted house in Scotland', stood near Grandtully in Perthshire. Built in 1806, it was the home of the Steuart family for over 400 years. Following the death of Major Robert Steuart in 1876, the house gained a reputation for being haunted: a ghostly nun was seen walking in the grounds and loud crashing noises as well as footsteps and the sound of unseen people quarrelling were heard by visitors. Major Steuart, a believer in reincarnation, claimed he would return to the house after death in the form of a dog, a proposition that upset surviving members of his family to the extent that they ordered all the dogs on the estate to be shot following his funeral. In 1896, following reports that a family who had taken on a twelve-month tenancy had fled after only eleven weeks because of strange and terrifying happenings, John Chrichton-Steuart, the 3rd Marquess of Bute, together with members of the recently formed Society for Psychical Research, carried out an on-site investigation but their results were inconclusive. In the 1960s it was suggested that the loud cracking noises and similar sounds reported at Ballechin over the years were the result of localised earthquakes and that the sighting of apparitions on the estate were the result of suggestion. The house was demolished following a fire in 1963.

An interesting variation on the 'most haunted' theme is Pluckley in Kent, said to be the most haunted village in England. Its numerous ghosts include a phantom highwayman who haunts the appropriately named Fright Corner; the spectre of a pipe-smoking gypsy watercress woman; the sound of a coach and the drumming of horses' hooves on the road to nearby Maltman's Hill; the apparition of a miller who only appears before a thunderstorm breaks over the village; a screaming man smothered to death in a trench collapse at the local brickworks; the hanging body of a suicide; 'The Colonel', another suicide who at one time was seen walking in the former Park Wood where he took his own life, subsequently turned into grazing land; and the 'Lady of Rose Court', yet another suicide who appears between 4 and 5 p.m., the time she drank a deadly draft made from poisonous berries. There is also a ghostly cavalier, a woman in white, and a phantom dog. Unexplained noises and mysterious lights have been reported from the Dering Chapel in the church of St Nicholas, while the figures of a brown-habited monk and a woman in modern dress have also been seen inside the building.

THE HAUNTED HOUSES OF AMERICA

As a relatively young country, the history of haunted houses in the United States of America is, out of necessity, focused on buildings and mansions erected over the last 200 years or so. Many American hauntings have a Civil War flavour and a number of the best-known cases are connected with violent crimes and murder.

The most famous American murder house haunting is the controversial 'Amityville Horror', which took place in a large Dutch-style colonial house in Ocean Avenue, Long Island in the mid-1970s. On the night of 13 November 1974,

Ronald 'Butch' DeFeo killed six members of his own family, including his parents, with a hunting rifle inside the house and was subsequently sentenced to life imprisonment. Three years later, writer Jay Anson published a book in which he claimed that the subsequent owners of 112 Ocean Avenue, the Lutz family, had been driven out of their home after a month by a violent and terrifying haunting. George and Kathy Lutz claimed to have encountered hooded monk-like figures, a demonic pig with fiery red eyes, pools of green slime, strange sounds and voices as well as clouds of supernatural flies. *The Amityville Horror* was subsequently turned into a successful film franchise and there have been several sequel books. However, the Lutzes' credibility suffered a major blow in 1979 when Ronald DeFeo's lawyer claimed the entire 'horror' was an organised hoax inspired by a drawn-out and wine-fuelled conversation he had with the couple in the kitchen of the house in 1977, and today – despite continued media attention and the assertions of paranormal researchers Ed and Lorraine Warren (*see* Chapter 13) – the haunting has been largely discredited.

On 16 January 1935, Arizona Donnie Barker, alleged leader of the famous Ma Barker gang, along with her son Fred Barker, was killed in an FBI shoot-out in an isolated house on the shore of Lake Weir in Ocklawaha, Florida. For several years, the Ternent family, who used the building as a holiday home, reported hearing footsteps and ghostly voices at night as well as the sounds of a group of people arguing and playing cards. The apparition of a woman, thought to be Ma Barker herself, was also seen sitting at the bottom of a bed combing her long hair.

One of the most famous modern American ghost photographs, known as the Pink Lady of Greencastle, was taken by ghost hunter Guy Winters at the abandoned O'Haire Mansion, a remote house built in the 1830s on the outskirts of Greencastle, Indiana. One night during a violent electrical storm, Winters visited the house with a friend and as well as making a video recording of the investigation, took several still photographs. On developing, several of these were found to contain the image of a ghostly glowing figure with a clearly human face framed in an upstairs window. The phantom is thought to be that of Irene O'Haire, a former resident, who lived and died in the building in the early twentieth century. The haunted house has since been demolished and the site turned into farmland.

The Edgar Allen Poe House and Museum at No. 203 AmityStreet in Baltimore, Maryland, where the famous writer lived between 1832 and 1835, is said to be haunted by the ghost of an old woman with grey hair. Visitors have also heard disembodied voices and other strange noises, particularly in the vicinity of Poe's former attic bedroom. Despite his association with the building, the ghost of the author of such horror classics as *The Fall of the House of Usher* and *The Pit and the Pendulum* has not made an appearance in his old home.

In 1891, the *San Francisco Examiner* reported on a haunted house case that took place in Oakville, Georgia, involving a tenant farming family named Walsingham, who took up residence in a rented property along the Savannah River. Not long after moving in, Mr Walsingham disposed of some bones (which may

or may not have been human) that were discovered inside the house, and in so doing appeared to precipitate a violent and disturbing series of events. Soon the family began experiencing strange happenings. Disembodied voices including groans, laughter and a distressing wailing sound were heard at all times of the day and night coming from under the floors, often sounding in the room where the Walsinghams gathered to eat their meals. The family dog became agitated at a certain spot in the ground-floor hallway and barked uncontrollably at something that only it could see; later the dog was found in the hallway with a broken neck, as though it had been struck down with a powerful blow. The family reported the appearance of a disembodied arm, which took hold of the youngest daughter when she was in the bathroom, and Mr Walsingham claimed to have been followed one night in the garden by an invisible person who left naked footprints in the mud alongside him. One evening during a dinner party, the family heard a loud groaning sound, followed by a torrent of what was later confirmed to be human blood, which began dripping down on to the dining table from the ceiling overhead. When several guests investigated the room above, they found it empty and the floor undisturbed. Soon the Walsinghams abandoned the house and moved away, after which a local man named Gunn spent a night on the premises. He claimed to have witnessed a glowing disembodied head and to have been attacked by an invisible presence. After this incident, the Oakville haunting reportedly stopped as mysteriously as it began.

On 4 August 1892, a gruesome double murder took place in a house in Fall River, Massachusetts. Andrew and Abby Borden were found bludgeoned to death with an axe inside their home at No. 92 Second Street. Their daughter Lizzie Borden was

famously acquitted for their killing and the crime remains a mystery to this day. The original house, now a bed and breakfast establishment and museum, is said to be haunted by the sound of a crying woman and the apparition of a Victorian lady who appears to tuck guests up in their beds at night.

☙ ☙ ☙

Sometimes it is not a house that is haunted by a spirit, but the house itself that is the ghost. There are a number of reports and stories of phantom buildings that both appear and disappear in mysterious circumstances.

In the autumn of 1926, two ladies, Miss Wynne and Miss Allington, were walking from the village of Rougham to Bradfield St George in Suffolk when they passed a large Georgian period house with a stuccoed front and a portico set in its own grounds surrounded by a high brick wall. Both commented on the attractiveness of the building as they carried on their way. A few months later, both women were walking the same route and as they approached the same spot, were stunned to find that there was no sign of the old house that they both had seen previously. The couple walked the route a number of times again but the Georgian house had simply vanished …

The former Elizabethan manor house at Knighton Gorges, near Newchurch on the Isle of Wight, was demolished in the early 1820s and today nothing of the original building remains. Ghost hunter Gay Baldwin has collected many accounts of paranormal phenomena connected with the area. On New Year's Eve 1915, Miss Ethel Hargrove claimed to have visited the site of the lost house accompanied by a friend and experienced a vision of the building as it would have appeared, as well as the sound of carriages arriving at the front door and the apparition of a man in eighteenth-century clothes. The ghost house is said to have made another appearance in the years before the Second World

War, when a young visitor to the island reported seeing figures who he assumed were attending a fancy-dress party in Georgian costumes through the windows.

Devon is a county that is particularly rich in stories of phantom houses. The Irish ghost hunter Elliott O'Donnell (*see* Chapter 13) claimed to have collected an account of a ghostly cottage near Chagford on the north-east rim of Dartmoor, which was seen by two ladies from London, who made arrangements to rent it the following summer. When they returned, they found the site littered with grass and rubble, which had clearly not been disturbed for many years. Another Dartmoor legend – which may possibly have given rise to the Chagford story – 'the Phantom Cottage of the Moor', involved three girls lost in the vicinity of Buckfastleigh who came across a lamp-lit cottage by the roadside in which an old couple sat warming themselves beside the fire. The vision abruptly vanished, leaving them in darkness, and on their return the next day, they found that the spot where the cottage had appeared was nothing but an overgrown ruin. There is also a phantom house at Cadleigh near Tiverton which is said to appear three times a year, while a friend of the folklorist Theo Brown claimed to have encountered a ghostly manor house while out riding at Doccombe near Moretonhampstead.

In November 1939, two sisters whose husbands were serving in France encountered a phantom house while out walking near the coastal village of Slapton in South Devon. In this instance one of the women, who lived in a house 1 mile outside the village, knew no such building existed, yet she and her sister both experienced a clear vision of a large manor house with arched doors on the front elevation among the trees of a disused orchard. Several other smaller buildings appeared at the side of the main house and all remained visible for around five minutes before gradually fading away. The site was in fact once occupied by a real building, Harleston Manor, which had been demolished many years before.

THE GHOSTS THAT CAME BACK TO WORK

As well as historic buildings and stately homes, there are many convincing reports of offices and factories being haunted, often by former employees whose spirits seem reluctant to leave their old places of work.

One evening in December 1969, George Poole, a worker at the Mobil oil refinery at Coryton in Essex, was standing near a water filtration unit when he heard footsteps approaching out of the darkness. Looking up, he saw the figure of a man wearing a boiler suit and steel safety helmet walking down the roadway towards him. Unsure what the workman was doing at that time when most of the regular staff had gone home for the day, Poole called out but received no reply. As he made his way towards the figure, it continued to walk towards him until when only a few yards separated the two men, the stranger simply vanished. The ghost was thought to be that of a former employee who was killed in an accident at the plant when it was owned by the Cory Brothers fuel distributors shortly after the Second World War.

A similar phenomenon to that experienced by George Poole took place at the former Whitbread Brewery in Oakley Road, Luton, in September 1978. Early one Saturday morning, Richard Horne, a shift engineer in charge of the brewery boiler house, was asked to work through the night in order to have steam available for bottling to begin at 6.00 a.m. A short while after the appointed time, Horne noticed that production had not started and decided to enquire when the work would begin so he could go home. As he climbed up a ladder into the bottling hall, the engineer saw a tall broad man with grey hair wearing blue overalls and carrying a spanner who was standing with his back to him on the other side of the conveyors. Horne called out but was ignored. Thinking he had not been heard, he walked forward and again asked the man if he knew when the bottling was going to start but similarly received no reply, at which point the man began to walk away. Annoyed that he was being ignored, Horne followed him with the intention of remonstrating with the worker for his rudeness, but at that moment the figure reached a solid bottle-washing machine and, appearing to pass through, instantly vanished. Dumfounded, Horne walked round to the other side of the machinery but the man was nowhere to be seen. Checking with the security gate, he found that the bottling was now starting later in the morning and that he and the security guard were at that time the only people present on the site. Unnerved by his experience, for some time Horne told no one except his wife; later, when he did tell other workers at the plant he was laughed at, but several colleagues later admitted that they had in fact seen a similar apparition on individual occasions. The ghost was identified as a former member of the maintenance team who had died of cancer. Today, the former Whitbread site has been turned into a housing estate.

Another incident of an employee's ghost being seen at his former place of work was collected by Bedfordshire ghost hunter, Tony Broughall, a former member of the Ghost Club and the Society for Psychical Research. On several occasions during 1970, office workers at the Chrysler UK truck factory in Boscombe Road, Dunstable, reported strange and inexplicable happenings: one worker complained of a disturbing 'presence' in one of the upper offices, guard dogs became unsettled while patrolling the building, doors were seen opening and closing by themselves, while the figure of a man wearing a dark blue pin-striped suit, observed at a desk seemingly engrossed in his work, suddenly vanished when approached by a cleaner. In 1974, the activity appeared to move to another part of the site known as the Ranch House, where lights were interfered with, despite no faults being found with the wiring. Broughall established that the ghost was that of a former office clerk who had died in late 1969 and, as well as the main Boscombe Road building, had also worked for a period of time in the Ranch House itself. Like the Luton brewery, the Chrysler site has also since been demolished.

3

GHOSTS OF CHURCHES, CHAPELS AND ABBEYS

Religious buildings, with their great age and unique associations with life, death and spirituality, are well known as haunted places. Cathedrals, abbeys, chapels and parish churches all have their ghost stories and while some are little more than colourful anecdotes, some hauntings are particularly convincing and well documented.

The ruined twelfth-century coastal church of St Mary's at Reculver in Kent is haunted by the eerie sound of a crying baby. Excavation work carried out during the 1960s uncovered several infant skeletons, which seem to support previous local legends of the ghosts of screaming children that are associated with the site.

In 1954, the Revd K.F. Lord took a photograph of the altar at the Church of Christ the Consoler in Skelton-cum-Newby, a Victorian building constructed in the grounds of Newby Hall in North Yorkshire. When the photograph was developed, the Revd Lord was astonished to see the tall figure of a cowled monk-like apparition superimposed on one side of the altar. The photograph remained unpublished until the 1960s and is now well known. There was no previous history of a haunting in the church and the vicar was adamant that both his camera and the photograph had not been tampered with.

Another ghostly monk, this time with a musical ear, haunts the Holy Trinity church at Caister-on-Sea near Great Yarmouth in Norfolk. One night in early 1967, a tape recorder left running by the vicar captured the sound of the organ being played inside the locked and empty building.

As well as its own spectral monk, which was seen walking down the aisle by a former dean, Carlisle Cathedral is haunted by the apparition of a Civil War cavalier and a dwarf-like figure with silver buckles on his shoes, the latter being seen by visitors in 1868. W.J. Phythian-Adams, a former Canon of Carlisle who became heavily involved in the investigation of Borley Rectory, was convinced that the ghost monk existed, but whether he himself saw the ghost is unclear.

One of the most bizarre and off-the-wall hauntings in the annals of British ghostlore is the phantom hole in the ground encountered by a Devonshire vicar in the late 1940s. In 1946, Revd Byles (later chaplain at Livery Dole in Exeter) and his wife took up the living at the church of St Bartholomew's in the remote village of Yealmpton, 6 miles east of Plymouth. One Saturday afternoon, the vicar and his wife both discovered a large hole approximately 3 yards wide and of an uncertain depth, which had appeared in the pathway leading away from the south door of the chancel. The couple were able to see what appeared to be part of a wall some feet below the ground and the hole's physical reality was easily confirmed when Revd Byles threw a stone into it. Assuming that subsidence had taken place, the vicar went into the village and fetched a Mr Knight, the local builder and undertaker, and brought him back to assess the hole and measure up for some planks to temporarily cover it over. However, when the two men returned to the churchyard, the Revd Byles was astonished to see that the deep hole had completely disappeared and the grass and pathway were just as they had always been. The couple left the parish in 1950 and later gave a written account of their experience to folklorist Theo Brown.

For many years a mysterious whistling sound was reported regularly from the vicinity of the Kitchener Memorial Chapel in St Paul's Cathedral in London. This was thought to be the ghost of a former parson, whose figure was sometimes seen as well as heard, following cathedral staff around before disappearing into a section of stone walling inside the chapel itself. A hidden doorway was subsequently revealed at the same spot by renovation work in the cathedral, which led to a concealed stairway up to the cathedral dome. After this work was completed, the whistling ghost was not heard or seen again.

London's Westminster Abbey is home to an eclectic mixture of haunting apparitions. They include a procession of black-clad monks, seen one night by a patrolling policeman; the figure of a First World War soldier who appears near to the tomb of the Unknown Warrior; the apparition of a Royalist cavalier; and 'Father Benedictus', a monk apparently murdered by thieves in the early fourteenth century. For good measure, the abbey at one time had an allegedly haunted clock (later moved to St Paul's Cathedral), which was said to strike out of order whenever an important member of the Royal Family was about to die.

The Cathedral Church of St Nicholas in the centre of Newcastle, Tyne and Wear, is haunted by the apparition of a knight in full armour along with the sound of its metallic footsteps. The phenomenon appears to be connected with the thirteenth-century effigy of an unnamed knight, possibly a member of the household of Edward I (Edward Longshanks) who was King of England 1272–1307, and which occupies an alcove in the west wall.

THE GHOSTS ON THE MARSHES

A strong candidate for the most haunted church in England was the fourteenth-century parish church of St Mary at Langenhoe, on the Essex marshes between Colchester and West Mersey. Between 1937 and 1959, Revd Ernest Merryweather, originally from the North of England, reported a wealth of strange and inexplicable happenings both inside the church and in the surrounding graveyard. Incidents ranged from poltergeist phenomena, such as the great west door being violently slammed shut on a still, windless day and objects disappearing only to be recovered elsewhere, to footsteps, knocks, thuds, bangs and the sound of disembodied chanting. Local legends tell of a 'lady in black' who walks around the church at night, while in 1908, two sisters reported seeing a nun-like figure which moved slowly along the path through the graveyard and disappeared into the north wall towards the west end of the church. Revd Merryweather also reported seeing ghostly figures, including a woman in modern dress who appeared while the rector was alone in the church playing the organ, and on another occasion two people dressed in medieval or Elizabethan clothing, seen during the course of a Sunday service. Closed for worship in the late 1950s, St Mary's – which had been damaged and later restored following the Essex earthquake of 1884 – stood abandoned and neglected before being finally demolished in 1962. Historically linked by its association with the Waldegrave family to the Manor of Borley and as a consequence its famous haunted rectory, perhaps it is no surprise that there were ghosts at Langenhoe. Ernest Merryweather, who died in 1965, also claimed to have had a particularly sensual encounter with the paranormal during his time at the parish when, in nearby Langenhoe Hall, he was briefly embraced by the unmistakable form of an invisible naked woman.

☙ ☙ ☙

A skeletal cyclist is said to haunt the roadway outside the former church of St Mary (now a museum) at Woodhorn in Northumberland.

In 1928, a Mrs Wickstead was on a motor tour of Worcestershire when she stopped off at All Saints' church in the village of Hollybush and photographed one of her companions, Mrs Laurie, in the churchyard. When the negative was developed some six weeks later, it showed the clear figures of an embracing couple standing on the path against the background of a yew tree, a spot known to have been deserted at the time. Mrs Wickstead corresponded with Sir Oliver Lodge concerning the photograph, which despite being later examined by the Society for Psychical Research, remains a mystery to this day.

The apparition of a ghostly monk, said to be a murder victim dating from the 1100s, haunts the Lady Chapel at Hereford Cathedral. It was seen by several witnesses in the roadway outside the cathedral during a festival in the 1950s.

The twelfth-century church of St Peter's at Babraham near Cambridge is haunted by at least four ghosts. On quiet weekdays, an invisible phantom possessing a magnificent soprano voice has 'often' been heard, while visitors have also reported a distinct feeling of not being alone and the unmistakable scent of expensive perfume. The figure of a woman in Victorian clothes has also been seen here.

In 1923, a strange image, said to be a likeness of John Liddel, the former Dean of Christ Church Cathedral, Oxford, appeared on an internal wall of the building and was seen by many people. It may still survive, concealed behind an altar that was constructed in the 1930s. Liddel himself died in 1898.

Now used as a conference centre, the former Hitchin Priory in Hertfordshire was occupied by White Friars before the Dissolution of the Monasteries. There are two ghosts here: a Grey Lady, seen in the grounds as recently as 1973, and the apparition of a Royalist officer named Goring, whose headless apparition is said to ride to the priory on the night of 15 June each year.

One of the north of England's most iconic ruins, Whitby Abbey is now closely associated with the world of vampires and the undead, thanks to its important role as the arrival point for Count Dracula in Bram Stoker's famous novel. Likewise, the abbey's ghosts are both imaginative and imbued with drama. A death coach pulled by headless horses is said to drive through the shell-like ruin and over the nearby East Cliff, vanishing before hitting the waves below; a phantom choir sings at dawn each 6 January, while a weeping nun, Constance de Beverly, walks near the steps leading to a twelfth-century passageway under the south transept. The oldest ghost is that of the first abbess, St Hilda, known as the White Lady, whose shrouded form has been seen on occasions silhouetted in the highest of the empty gaping windows.

4

HAUNTED CASTLES
AND PALACES

Beginning with ancient hillforts and progressing through Roman fortifications and on to the massive battlemented and towered buildings of the conquering Normans, castles – like churches – are an integral part of the history and development of our islands, and continue to exert a commanding influence on the psyche of the British people. Fortunately, days of dark deeds, murder and bloodshed – echoes of which have undoubtedly seeped into the stones and masonry of their massive walls and towers – are now gone, but over many years down to the present day, reports and continued experiences show that the inexplicable forces of the haunting world can still bring these times, at least for brief moments, back to life.

Two colourful female ghosts haunt Stirling Castle, an imposing twelfth-century cliff-top fortress constructed at the head of the Firth of Forth, 30 miles north-west of Edinburgh. An appearance of the Green Lady, thought to be either an attendant of Mary, Queen of Scots or the daughter of a former castle governor who committed suicide after her fiancé was killed in a shooting accident, is considered to be an omen of impending disaster. Her silent figure has been reported over many years, and presents herself as a misty apparition that appears suddenly beside the unsuspecting witness before vanishing in equally mysterious circumstances. Stirling is also haunted by a Pink Lady, a figure in a pink dress that has been glimpsed walking in the vicinity of the Chapel Royal, which may

perhaps be Mary herself; she was crowned Mary I of Scotland here on 9 September 1543.

An impressive roster of ghosts makes Conwy Castle one of the most haunted castles in Wales. As well as an unidentified figure wrapped in a cloak which haunts the ramparts, visitors and staff have encountered a misty form inside the King's Tower dungeon, a hooded monk in the Queen's Garden, a girl in a flower-patterned dress in the Inner Ward, and a dark apparition, possibly that of a soldier or guard, standing in the King's Tower itself.

The haunting of Bramber Castle, a ruinous motte and bailey fortification overlooking the River Adur in West Sussex, brings to mind the celebrated ghost stories of English academic Montague Rhodes James, in particular his eerie classic, *Lost Hearts*, first published in 1904. As in James' story, the ghosts of Bramber are two wretched children, emaciated and dressed in rags, which have been seen from time to time amongst the castle ruins. They are thought to be the sons of William de Braose, a descendant of the original founder, who along with William's wife were starved to death in Windsor Castle by King John in the early thirteenth century. They are most often seen at Christmas time, their hands held out as if begging for food before quickly fading from sight, a psychic echo of a cruel and violent past.

Many ghost hunters have become fascinated with the queen of haunted castles, Glamis in Angus, Scotland, the history of which is intertwined with legend, folklore and the paranormal. The childhood home of Queen Elizabeth, the Queen Mother, Glamis is famous for stories of a hidden chamber, said to conceal

a hideously deformed member of the Bowes-
Lyon family (the Monster of Glamis),
a vampire servant caught in the act of
sucking blood from a victim, and the
tale of 'Earl Beardie', who played
cards on the Sabbath with the Devil.
The figure of a woman in grey has
been seen kneeling in the chapel and
a white lady haunts the grounds
where a fast-moving spectre known
as Jack the Runner also appears.
Other ghosts include a figure in
armour, a tall apparition in a long coat,
and a little black boy who has been observed sitting on
a stone next to the door leading to the former Queen Mother's
sitting room.

☠ ☠ ☠

A headless drummer boy haunts the ramparts of Dover Castle in
Kent, while at Berry Pomeroy near Totnes in Devon, the ghosts
of two doomed lovers who meet in the gatehouse share the ruins
with the apparition of a woman in old-fashioned clothing: this is
the sinister ghost of Lady Margaret Pomeroy, said to have been
starved to death here by her sister Eleanor, who now entices
unwary visitors down into the dungeon where she met her fate
many years ago.

Corby Castle, on the outskirts of Carlisle, is haunted by
a famous ghost known as the Radiant Boy, first seen by the
Rector of Greystoke during a visit in 1803. After retiring to bed,
the rector found himself awake in the early hours of the morning.
As he looked around the empty bedroom, he became aware
of a glimmer of light, which quickly increased in brightness
to the point that the clergyman thought that the bedclothes

had somehow caught on fire. As he made to rouse himself, the rector was astonished to see the glowing figure of a young boy, dressed in white with golden locks, standing beside the bed. The apparition was visible for several minutes before turning and gliding towards the fireplace where it disappeared, taking its radiant light with it. The origins of the Radiant Boy, who was last seen at the castle in 1834, are unclear.

GHOSTLY KINGS AND QUEENS

On the night of 21 September 1327, King Edward II was murdered in a cell at Berkeley Castle in Gloucestershire on the orders of his wife Queen Isabella, who had become the lover of Roger de Mortimer, 3rd Baron Mortimer and 1st Earl of March. Edward had been imprisoned for several months and his wife had become impatient that the austere conditions in the castle dungeons had not weakened the monarch to the point that he would expire through natural causes. The king's death was brutal in the extreme: reports suggest that as well as being suffocated, the deposed Edward was held with his legs spread apart and a red-hot iron or poker was thrust up into his rectum. There is a tradition at Berkeley that his agonised screams have imprinted themselves in the massive walls and stones of the ancient building and at times can be heard again, particularly in the vicinity of the room in which Edward is thought to have been held captive.

The reign of Henry VIII (1509–1547), the most famous and recognisable king of England, born at Greenwich on 28 June 1491, has provided the country's ghostlore with many

interesting and enduring phantoms and supernatural stories. Henry died in the Palace of Whitehall in 1547 and is buried in St George's Chapel at Windsor Castle, Berkshire. It is here that his shuffling ghost is said to walk, groaning in pain as he drags an ulcerated leg behind him.

Henry's multiple marriages, six well-known unions together spanning thirty-eight years between June 1509 and his death in 1547, have given a number of English castles and palaces several high-profile royal hauntings. The most prolific of these is the ghost of Anne Boleyn, Henry's second wife, who met her end on the scaffold at the Tower of London on 19 May 1536, beheaded with a single stroke of the sword, her executioner having been brought over from France specifically for the occasion. In the years following her death, Anne has reputedly been seen on several occasions and at multiple locations, both with and without her head. At Blicking Hall in Norfolk, where Anne may have been born in the early 1500s, her headless spectre, with her severed head resting in her lap, is said to return to the house at midnight on each anniversary of her death, riding in a phantom coach pulled and driven by equally headless horses and coachmen. Anne also haunts Hever Castle in Kent, where on Christmas Eve her apparition crosses the River Eden over a bridge in the castle grounds; it was in these same gardens that she first met Henry VIII in 1522. St Peter and St Paul's church at Salle in Norfolk, which has strong links with the Boleyn family, is another reputed haunting ground, as is Hampton Court Palace in south-west London, where she was reported as appearing in a pale blue dress by palace servants towards the end of the 1800s. The location where it seems she

most often appears (and for which more than anecdotal evidence exists) is – perhaps not surprisingly – the Tower of London. In 1864, a soldier from the King's Royal Rifle Corps was court-martialed after being found in a stupor one night next to his sentry post outside the entrance to the King's House. He claimed in his defence that he had challenged an approaching figure and was so shocked when he realised that it was in fact a headless woman walking towards him that he collapsed in a faint. Interestingly, two other soldiers gave evidence at his trial and also testified to seeing a similar apparition, thought to be the ghost of Anne Boleyn walking near to the site where she was executed, and the soldier was therefore acquitted and restored to his regiment. Anne has also been seen walking in the aisle of the Chapel of St Peter ad Vincula (St Peter in Chains) at the tower, and her appearance is traditionally considered to herald an approaching death within the tower precinct. She was last seen during the Second World War, shortly before the German spy, Josef Jakobs, was executed by a firing squad drawn from soldiers of the Scots Guards just after 7 a.m. on 15 August 1941.

Hampton Court, the beautiful Tudor palace built by Cardinal Thomas Wolsey in the early sixteenth century and later given as a gift to Henry VIII shortly before Wolsey's death in 1530, is haunted by another two of Henry's wives: Jane Seymour and Catherine Howard. The gentle ghost of Jane Seymour, who was proclaimed Queen of England on 4 June 1536, just over a fortnight after the execution of Anne Boleyn, walks silently near the stairway leading to the Silver Stick Gallery. She has been described as a tall figure with an eerily shining face, dressed in white with a long train behind her and carrying a lighted candle, the flame of which never flickers. A cyclical phantom, Queen Jane is reported to appear most often on or around 12 October, the date on which she gave birth to her son, Edward VI. She died only days later at Hampton Court on 24 October 1537 from an infection brought on by a particularly difficult labour. The silent

spectre of Jane Seymour is a far cry from the
screaming ghost of the tragic Catherine Howard,
who traditionally appears in what is now known
as the Haunted Gallery, a corridor leading to
the palace chapel, along which she was dragged
shrieking and begging for mercy by the palace
guards on 4 November 1541 after attempting
to plead with the king for her life. Catherine
had been stripped of her title after being charged
with adultery and treason following an affair with Thomas
Culpeper, one of Henry's courtiers. She was beheaded at the
Tower of London on 13 February 1542.

As well as Henry VIII, Windsor Castle, originally built by
William the Conqueror and much altered and expanded down
through the centuries, is also known for three other royal ghosts.
Charles I, beheaded in the grounds of the Palace of Whitehall
on 30 January 1649, was subsequently buried in the castle's
St George's Chapel a few days later and it is to Windsor that his
ghost is said to return; his sad-looking figure has been seen most
often in the Canon's House, a building in the castle grounds.
On the day following his execution, the deposed monarch's head
was sewn back on to his body, which is perhaps why Charles'
ghost appears complete and unmutilated. Henry VIII's daughter,
Elizabeth I, known variously as 'The Virgin Queen' and 'Good
Queen Bess', died at Richmond in Surrey on 24 March 1603,
aged sixty-nine. She is buried with her half-sister, Mary I, in
a tomb in Westminster Abbey. Despite this, it is to Windsor
Castle (particularly the Queen's Library, once part of the royal
apartments) that her ghost is known to have returned on
occasion in the past, dressed in black and with a black lace scarf
over her hair and shoulders. Another monarch who walks the
apartments he knew in life is George III, the 'Mad King' who
lived at Windsor from the time that his eldest son ruled as
prince regent in 1811 until his death at the age of eighty-one

in January 1820. His bearded apparition was seen soon after by several castle soldiers during the ceremony of the changing of the guard, standing at the window of his room below the castle library, raising his hand to acknowledge the salute as he had done many times in the past, despite his ultimately incurable mental confusion.

Another King George, in this instance the 'Mad King's' grandfather, George II, haunts Kensington Palace, today the official London residence of the Duke and Duchess of Cambridge. Born in Hanover in 1683, the king reportedly spent his last days watching a weather vane on the palace roof, hoping to see it swing and signal the approach of ships bringing dispatches from his beloved homeland of Germany. The king died from an aneurysm on 25 October 1760 and tradition has it that when the wind blows strongly across the rooftops of Kensington Palace, his grey face can be seen reflected in the window glass of his former apartment, looking again at the palace weather vane, this time from beyond the grave.

5

GHOSTS OF
STAGE AND SCREEN

The empty stage, shadowy auditorium and lofty fly towers and galleries of the playhouse combined with the unique atmosphere of theatreland provide a ready-made environment for tales of ghosts and spectres. As well as being an integral part of some of the stage's finest dramas, actors invariably tread the boards with many real-life ghosts and practically all of our theatres have traditional stories of hauntings and strange happenings.

Two former theatrical managers haunt the Haymarket Theatre in London's West End, a playhouse whose origins date back to the early decades of the eighteenth century. When doors backstage mysteriously open and close of their own accord, it is generally assumed that David Edward Morris, who co-managed the theatre with his brother-in-law, George Colman, and later became sole manager in 1817, is paying those present a visit. Morris was unpopular with the theatre artistes and is said to have died of a broken heart following the premature death of his daughter. The Haymarket's best-known ghost is the Victorian actor-manager and comedian, John Baldwin Buckstone, who ran the theatre for twenty-five years and died in 1879 aged seventy-seven, a year after relinquishing the job he loved. His apparition, dressed in a long black frock coat, has been seen by stagehands and several actors and actresses over the years including Meriel Forbes, Drusilla Wills, Margaret Rutherford, and most recently *Star Trek: The Next Generation* and *X-Men* actor, Sir Patrick Stewart, who claimed to have seen Buckstone standing in the wings during a performance of Samuel Beckett's *Waiting for Godot* in 2009.

The Coliseum in St Martin's Lane, which opened in 1904 – the first London theatre to be equipped with electric lighting and boasting the widest proscenium arch in the capital – was said at one time to be haunted by the apparition of a First World War soldier which appeared in the dress circle walkway just before the house lights were about to be lowered for a performance. The ghost, which walked towards a seat in the second row before disappearing, was thought to be a soldier killed in action in France in October 1918 who had spent his last evening at the Coliseum on leave.

Of all London's theatres, the Theatre Royal in Drury Lane is considered to be the most haunted. A playhouse has existed on the site since the mid-seventeenth century and there have been several buildings. After a previous incarnation was destroyed by fire in 1809, the current theatre first opened on 10 October 1812 with a production of *Hamlet*. The theatre's most famous ghost is the Man in Grey, thought to be a former actor, who appears in the upper circle dressed in a tricorn hat and a long grey cloak and complete with white wig and a sword. The theatre historian W.J. MacQueen-Pope (1888–1960) claimed to have seen him on several occasions during afternoon matinees, while in 1938, a cleaner working in the upper circle during a rehearsal saw a man sitting in a seat in the fourth row looking down on to the stage, who vanished as she went across to speak to him. The ghost made another appearance in 1950 when Morgan Davies, the lead in the musical *Carousel*, described seeing a cloaked and semi-transparent figure standing in one of the boxes while he was performing on stage. On this occasion, the figure was visible for at least ten minutes before disappearing. This particular phantom is thought to be that of a murder victim whose skeleton was discovered concealed inside an alcove during alteration work in 1848, and a sighting of the Man in Grey is considered to be a sign of good luck to a production and its cast. The Theatre Royal's other ghosts include actor Charles Macklin (1699–1797) who accidentally killed a fellow actor in an argument over a wig in the theatre's Scene Room in 1735, the clown Joseph Grimaldi (1778–1837) who is thought to be the unseen person guiding nervous actors on to the stage from time to time, and comedian Dan Leno (1860–1904), another comedy actor. Stanley Lupino, father of Hollywood actress Ida Lupino, claimed to have seen Leno's ghost in his dressing room one night after a show.

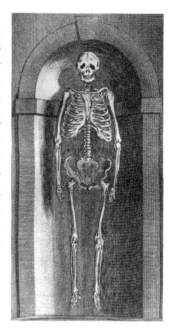

The Theatre Royal, Bradford, is traditionally haunted by the ghost of Sir Henry Irving, the first actor to receive a knighthood and often considered to have inspired Bram Stoker to create the fictional character of Count Dracula. Irving suffered a stroke while on stage at the theatre on 13 October 1905 and died shortly afterwards. He was sixty-seven.

HAUNTED HOLLYWOOD

Some of the biggest names in the electric theatre of the cinema have seemingly come back from beyond the grave after taking their final bows here on earth. In 1962, the famous Hollywood actor John Wayne bought the USS *YMS-328*, a decommissioned United States Navy minesweeper, which had been converted into a luxury private yacht. Wayne renamed the ship *Wild Goose* and owned it up until his death on 11 June 1979. It is to the

Wild Goose that his ghost is said to return, revisiting the vessel he loved in life. Later owners have reported hearing inexplicable footsteps and 'The Duke's' apparition, a misty grey silhouette, has been seen on several occasions. The yacht, seemingly with Wayne's ghost still aboard, was included on the American National Register of Historic Places in 2011 and is now owned by a private cruise company.

The credit for the most travelled and prolific film star ghost must go to silent screen star Rudolph Valentino, whose roles in early classics such as *The Sheik* (1921), *Blood and Sand* (1922) and *The Eagle* (1925) made him one of the cinema's first true sex symbols. Thousands mourned his death from acute peritonitis in New York on 23 August 1926, aged thirty-one. Since then, Valentino's ghost has been reportedly encountered at over fifteen locations in Southern California, many of which have personal connections with the tragic actor. As well as Falcon's Lair, his former mansion home in Bella Drive, Beverley Hills, Valentino is also said to have revisited the Beach House at Cahuenga Street in Oxnard, where he stayed during the filming of *The Sheik*; the Santa Maria Inn; the old Knickerbocker Hotel in Ivar Avenue, Los Angeles; and the Hollywood Hotel on Hollywood Boulevard. The silent star also rides one of his favourite horses along Will Rogers State Beach, dressed in white robes and with a rose between his teeth, while for good measure his pet dog, Kabar, haunts the LA Pet Cemetery in Old Scandia Lane, Calabasas.

Actress and singer Marilyn Monroe, one of the most famous pop culture icons of all time, was found dead at her home at No. 12305 Fifth Helena Drive in Brentwood, Los Angeles, on 5 August 1962; she was thirty-six years old. The surroundings of her death from a drugs overdose remain shrouded in mystery, something that her ghost has shed little light on. Marilyn's apparition has reportedly been seen on several occasions reflected in a full-length mirror in the Hollywood Roosevelt Hotel on

Roosevelt Boulevard, where she lived for a time in Suite 1200. She is also said to haunt her gravesite at the Westwood Memorial Park Cemetery in Glendon Avenue, Los Angeles, as well as the penthouse suite at the Beverly Hilton.

❧ ❧ ❧

In January 1966, Alfred Tanner, a painter and decorator, was contracted to paint the auditorium of the Theatre Royal in Margate, the oldest theatre in the county of Kent and the second oldest playhouse in Britain. In order to minimise any inconvenience in the running of the theatre, it was agreed that the work would be carried out between 10 p.m. and 6.30 a.m. the following day. Tanner was not a local man and was unaware that the Royal had (and still has) a haunted reputation stretching back over 100 years. Soon after beginning work on the first night, the decorator became aware of the sound of voices and unusual whispering sounds. This continued during the second night and was accompanied by the sound of slamming doors and footsteps. Suspecting a practical joke, he was about to issue a challenge when he saw a disembodied head, like that of a woman with frizzy hair, two slits for eyes and a thin receding chin, which came round the curtains on the left of the stage and drifted across to the other side before fading from sight. Tanner refused to work in the theatre alone again and later recognised the face from a photograph which was hanging on one of the staircases: it was actress-manager Sarah Thorne, who had run the Royal for over thirty years before her death on 27 February 1899, aged sixty-two.

Stories of ghosts at Gloucester's Kings Theatre date back to the mid-1960s. In 1965, a local newspaper, *The Citizen*, reported the sound of footsteps being heard walking in deserted parts of the building, particularly at the rear of the stage and in rooms in the wings on either side. The theatre was originally a meeting hall for the Salvation Army and it is thought that a figure seen there by one of the costume makers late one night may be a former Salvation Army captain. A Mr Raybould claimed to have seen the figure of a man in ordinary working clothes hovering nearly 2ft above the wooden stage, which remained visible for several seconds before vanishing: the original stage level was much higher during the time that General Booth's 'soldiers' were resident.

The ghost of a railway signalman named Henry Wilkins haunts the Station Theatre, an amateur dramatics venue in West Town on Hayling Island in Hampshire. The haunting dates from the time that the building was used as a goods shed on the old Hayling Billy line, which was closed to all rail traffic in 1962 when the cost of replacing a swing bridge across Langstone Harbour proved too expensive to carry out. The apparition of a man has been reported in the derelict goods yard on a number of occasions beginning shortly after the line was shut and at varying intervals during the 1970s and 1980s. Soon after the Station Theatre opened in 1996, the ghost returned and was seen walking around inside the building.

There are also ghosts at the New Alexandra Theatre, Birmingham, haunted by a former manager; the Grand Theatre, Blackpool, where poltergeist activity has been reported; the Haymarket Theatre, Leicester, haunted by the apparition of a little boy dressed in a sailor's suit; and Wimbledon Theatre, which has at least two ghosts: that of former manager, J.B. Mulholland, and a laughing lady in grey who amuses herself by vanishing through closed doors.

6

POLTERGEISTS AND
OTHER VIOLENT GHOSTS

oltergeists are amongst the most recorded and prolific of all
ghosts. There are literally hundreds of accounts, both ancient
and modern. In most cases, these poltergeist hauntings start
up unexpectedly and last for a few weeks before stopping as
mysteriously as they began. Some cases have been known to last
longer, sometimes for several months and on rare occasions for
several years. All cultures, countries and generations have reports
of ghostly activity that, today, researchers and investigators
would classify as being poltergeist cases.

☠ ☠ ☠

Poltergeist outbreaks are known to follow a set pattern of events.
Poltergeists begin by making knocking or rapping sounds, which
are heard coming from walls and floors. This is often followed
by the movement of furniture and other household objects.
Often, small objects such as stones, coins and similar items are
thrown about: objects are frequently observed in flight but rarely
are they actually seen to move by themselves. These poltergeist
projectiles are often found to be warm to the touch when they
are immediately picked up. Sometimes, fragile items such as light
bulbs can be hurled about without being damaged.

Fire and water are often features of poltergeist outbreaks.
Poltergeists often create pools of water, which are found on

floors and tables. They are described as being perfectly circular in shape. Spontaneous localised fires can also take place. Electrical equipment such as television sets, electric kettles and telephones often overload or malfunction.

Some poltergeists try to communicate with the people they are haunting. Sometimes this can be a knocking code – one knock for 'yes', two knocks for 'no' – while on other occasions, letters and words are found written on pieces of paper or on walls and doors. Sometimes poltergeists are known to whistle and people have reported hearing voices coming out of the air.

The vast majority of poltergeist cases involve the movement and manipulation of objects and it is rare that actual 'ghosts' or apparitions are reported. In some instances, people have reported seeing phantom figures, and in some rare cases, strange animals have also been seen.

☙ ☙ ☙

The Bealings Bells is a name given to a poltergeist outbreak that occurred in the village of Great Bealings, near Woodbridge, Suffolk in 1834. Major Edward Moore, a retired Indian Army officer and his family, were plagued by an invisible force which rang the servant bells in their house at all times of the day and night. The disturbances began on 2 February and lasted nearly two months. Moore investigated the happenings himself and subsequently published a book on the case. In 1965, Trevor Hall, a sceptical researcher, made a study of the Bealings Bells and concluded that Major Moore had been tricked by one of his staff playing practical jokes. Despite this, the case has all the hallmarks of a classic poltergeist outbreak and remains a mystery.

'Scratching Fanny' was the name of the poltergeist that had most of London in uproar and caused crowds of sightseers to flock to a house close to Smithfield market in the shadow of St Paul's Cathedral in 1762. Also known as the Cock Lane Ghost, the disturbances attracted the attention of none other than Dr Johnson, who – along with a committee that comprised other notables such as Lord Dartmouth Aldrich and John Douglas, Bishop of Salisbury – came to the conclusion that the haunting was a hoax perpetrated by a clerk named Richard Parsons in an attempt to frame a licentious moneylender named William Kent for murder. Parsons and a number of other conspirators were later sent to prison. However, in its early stages, which involved knocks and raps before the death of Fanny Lynes (William Kent's sister-in-law), who later was alleged to have returned to haunt the house, the case of the Cock Lane Ghost may well have involved some genuine poltergeist-type phenomena.

An early nineteenth-century American poltergeist haunting is the strange case now known as the Bell Witch. The story, for which several anecdotal versions exist, has been the inspiration for several modern films and stories, most notably *The Blair Witch Project* (1999) and *An American Haunting* (2005). Although now consigned by most researchers to folklore, some aspects of the Bell Witch have parallels with other well-documented poltergeist cases, particularly the appearance of strange apparitional animals and similar creatures which were a prominent feature of the haunting of Willington Mill on Tyneside (*see* Chapter 9). John and Mary Bell were successful farmers who lived with their eight children on a 1,000-acre holding near the town of Adams, Tennessee. The family were staunch Baptists and were held in high regard by the local community. However, an outbreak of strange and unprecedented disturbances began some time in 1817, which lasted for several years. Knocks, raps and gnawing sounds, as well as other scratching and scraping noises, were heard inside the Bell farmhouse at all times of the day and night. The Bell children were scratched and slapped in bed and as the haunting progressed, the family heard at first whistling noises and then a voice which gave many contradictory statements as to its identity: at first the poltergeist claimed to be a nature spirit which had been alive for millions of years, then the spirit of a person who lay buried in the woods near the farm, then later still the ghost of an immigrant slave as well as a witch summed by a local woman, Kate Batts, with whom John Bell had fallen out over a business deal. At one point, the haunting is said to have come to the attention of General Andrew Jackson (1767–1845) who later became the seventh President of the United States. He visited the farm with an exorcist but the phenomena persisted and most versions of the story describe the Bell Witch moving around other farms in the area, where it caused similar mischief and unpleasantness. John Bell died in December 1820, after which the ghost, 'Kate', announced it would leave the family alone for seven years. After returning for a fortnight in 1828, 'Kate' made another promise to depart, this time for 107 years. By the time this anniversary came round, a Tennessee journalist, Matin V. Ingram, had written a book, *An Authenticated History of the Famous Bell Witch* (1894), on which many of today's versions are based. The Bell Witch Cave near the Red River on the former Bell Farm is today a popular tourist attraction which has developed a ghostlore all of its own: according to several accounts, accidents and misfortune befall anyone rash enough to take away stones or similar artefacts from inside. Reports of these incidents have been collected by American ghost hunter Troy Taylor.

The case of the Stratford Poltergeist took place in Connecticut in 1850. Twelve-year-old Harry Phelps was dumped in a water cistern and found suspended from a tree. His mother was also pinched and pricked with a needle, while on one occasion a full bottle of ink was thrown over her as she was about to leave on a family excursion.

The Great Amhurst Mystery was an important American haunting, described by psychical researcher Nandor Fodor as 'one of the most famous poltergeist cases in the world', aspects of which may have influenced some of the reported phenomena at Borley Rectory. Daniel Teed, a shoe factory foreman, his wife, Olive, and their two children, as well as several close relatives – Daniel's brother plus Olive's own brother and her two sisters – all lived at No. 6 Princes Street, a yellow-painted wooden house in Amhurst, Nova Scotia. The whole family were active members of the Wesleyan Methodist church, but between September 1878 and July 1879, they became involved in a violent and protracted haunting, at the centre of which was nineteen-year-old Esther Cox, Olive Teed's unmarried sister. An assault and attempted rape on Esther was the catalyst that set into motion an increasingly violent and unsettling explosion of psychic phenomena: bedclothes and mattresses along with their occupants were thrown on to the floor, raps and loud tapping noises sounded throughout the house, objects were thrown and messages were found scribbled on the walls. On several occasions, Esther Cox's body began swelling up to twice its normal size and during these episodes, loud booming noises like thunderclaps sounded inside the house. There were also mysterious and unexplained voices and a number of small spontaneous fires that took place. The Teeds believed that Esther had become possessed by an evil spirit and the growing notoriety resulted in an investigation being carried out by a young actor, Walter Hubbell, who later wrote a bestselling book about his experiences and Esther Cox's phenomena. The haunting ceased as unexpectedly as it had begun and in later years Esther refused to talk about the happenings in case it invited the ghost to return.

The first Battersea Poltergeist phenomenon took place in a Victorian terraced house in Eland Road, Lavender Hill, in early 1928 and was reported widely in the London press. At the height of public interest in the story, mounted police were employed to keep back crowds of sightseers who thronged to Battersea to catch a glimpse of the haunting. This complex case was investigated by a pre-Borley Rectory Harry Price, who paid his first visit to the house on 28 January 1928. The household comprised an elderly invalid, Henry Robinson, his twenty-seven-year-old son Frederick, his two daughters, Lillah and Kate, who were both schoolteachers, a widow, Mrs Perkins, and her fourteen-year-old son, Peter. The Robinsons reported a lengthy catalogue of destructive phenomena that had commenced at the end of November 1927: numerous lumps of coal and soda, as well as several pennies had rained down on the conservatory roof, a pile of red-hot cinders had mysteriously appeared in the outhouse, loud banging and knocking sounds had been heard inside the house, furniture had overturned and windows had been broken. Mrs Perkins claimed that the dining-room chairs had marched down the hallway by themselves and it soon became necessary to remove Henry Robinson to a local infirmary for his own safety. The police, who suspected Frederick Robinson of causing the disturbances, at one point took him to St John's Hospital for a psychiatric examination but objects continued to move in his absence and he was later discharged. Not long after, Henry Robinson died and the family including Mrs Perkins and her son left Eland Road, after which the 'haunting' came to an end. Harry Price, who witnessed some phenomena inside the house, felt certain aspects of the case may have been genuine, although some of the stone and coal throwing appear to have been the work of inmates from a private asylum in an adjacent property, with whose owners the Robinsons had at one time fallen out. In 1941, Frederick Robinson gave an interview to the *Two Worlds* Spiritualist magazine and claimed that during the disturbances he had received messages from the poltergeist written using a pin on scraps of paper. The ghost signed itself as 'Tom Blood' and claimed he had been alive during the reign of William the Conqueror.

The second Battersea Poltergeist resided in a house in Wycliffe Road in 1956 and affected a fifteen-year-old schoolgirl named Shirley Hitchins. The disturbances began with the unexpected and mysterious appearance of a household key unknown to the family, which was found lying on the girl's bed. Mr Hitchins described the object as dropping from the ceiling as if out of nowhere. Knocks, rappings and other noises were heard in her presence, both at home in Battersea and subsequently at a West End department store where she started work as a dress cutter; her bus journey to and from the store was also disturbed by rapping sounds from the seat on which she sat. Using a knocking code, the Hitchins seemingly made contact with the poltergeist (which Shirley had named 'Donald') who claimed to be Louis Capet, the illegitimate son of Charles II of France. 'Donald' later wrote a letter to ghost hunter Andrew Green (1927–2004) who was called in to investigate by the *News Chronicle* newspaper, but it quickly became apparent that in fact Shirley Hitchins was the writer. The family also reported the uncontrollable movement of furniture and other household objects, the bedclothes were seen to be pulled and tugged from the bed in which Shirley was sleeping, and on one occasion she was seen lying rigid and levitating just over 6in from the surface of the mattress. The disturbances, which lasted in total for around two years, suddenly stopped as suddenly as they had begun. The original street, including the poltergeist house itself (No. 63), was demolished in the early 1970s. A book on the case, co-authored by Shirley Hitchins herself, appeared in 2013.

SOME HISTORICAL POLTERGEISTS

The ancient records known as the *Annales Fuldenses* or *Annals of Fulda* contain an account of the Bingen Poltergeist, which was recorded near Kempten in present-day Bavaria around AD 856–858. A farmer was plagued by a stone-throwing ghost who shock the walls of his house, set his crops alight and also shouted obscenities and accusations of improper behaviour as he walked around the village.

An examination of historical records has revealed many curious incidents from the past that today would be classed as exhibiting some form of poltergeist activity. They include poltergeists from China in AD 900; Istanbul, Turkey, in 1100; Le Mans, France, around 1135; Orielton in Pembrokeshire in 1184; Dagworth, Suffolk, in 1189; Stommeln near Cologne, in 1260; Eistett, near Nuremberg, around 1414, and many others.

In 1695, the house of stonemason Andrew Mackie and his family, who lived at Ringcroft in the parish of Rerrick near Dumfries in Scotland, was invaded by a violent stone-throwing poltergeist. Stones rained down on the family both day and night, although it became clear that the resident ghost respected the Sabbath, as all was quiet on a Sunday. The disturbances continued in earnest for the rest of the week, however, and as the weeks progressed became more violent and frightening: Mr Mackie was thrown out of bed on to the floor, had his hair pulled and was beaten about the head with a wooden stave. On one occasion, the children of the house noticed what appeared to be a person sitting beside the fire wrapped in one of their blankets; when the youngest child, a ten year old, ran forward and pulled at the blanket, it came away and there was nothing under it except a four-legged stool. A group of five local ministers who came to the house to exorcise the ghost were pelted with stones for their trouble. The disturbances began in February 1695 and lasted until 1 May. In the last week of April, the Ringcroft poltergeist changed tactics and, instead of throwing stones, began setting the house on fire. A strange black cloud, like a living thing, was seen inside one of the rooms, and threw mud and barley chaff in the faces of the Mackie family and their neighbours. On the first day of May, a small outbuilding used as a sheep pen burst into flames but none of the animals inside were injured. It was to be the final outrage, as the poltergeist disappeared immediately afterwards.

Shortly before Christmas 1771, Mrs Golding, an elderly woman living in the Stockwell district of London, took on a new maid, twenty-year-old Ann Robinson. It was a decision Mrs Golding was to regret, as Ann brought with her a destructive poltergeist now known as the 'Stockwell Ghost'. Knocks and violent noises broke out all over the house, plates were smashed, a clock was thrown down the stairs, a pestle and mortar jumped 6ft into the air, and eggs were thrown across the kitchen, hitting a cat on the head. Mrs Golding moved to the house of her niece, Mrs Pain, and then to the house of a neighbour, but the violent commotion continued. Unable to take any more of the ghostly violence, Mrs Golding gave Ann the sack, after which the phenomena ceased immediately.

A famous English poltergeist, known as 'Old Jeffrey', haunted Epworth Rectory in Lincolnshire, in the early years of the eighteenth century. For two months beginning on 1 December 1716, Epworth, home to the religious reformers John and Charles Wesley, the founders of Methodism, was plagued with a bewildering array of paranormal phenomena that has made the case one of the best-authenticated ghost stories amongst the early hauntings for which good reports survive. Mysterious knockings and eerie groaning noises began emanating from the rectory dining room while, at night, the Wesley children claimed to hear the footsteps of an unseen person who ascended and descended the stairs; furniture began moving by itself; a bed levitated into the air while the children lay on the mattress (a phenomenon witnessed by several visitors invited to the house to experience the strange happenings for themselves); an apparition dragging a long white robe across the floor was seen; and when Revd Samuel Wesley challenged the ghost to stop frightening the family and meet him in his study man to man, the study door was slammed shut with a powerful force. After several weeks, the Wesley family had become used to their invisible intruder and were no longer scared of it, at which point the disturbances at Epworth abruptly ceased.

Another famous poltergeist linked with religion, in this instance the founding of Modern Spiritualism, took place in Hydesville, near Rochester, New York, in 1848. The small, cabin-like house of the Fox family was invaded by a rapping ghost which became known as 'Mr Splitfoot' after a common local name for the Devil. A trio of young sisters, Leah, Margaret and Kate Fox, found they could communicate with the poltergeist and eventually became some of the world's first professional mediums. It was widely believed that the poltergeist was the spirit of a peddler who had been murdered and buried in the cellar of the house several years before. In 1904, bones were recovered from the house that appeared to substantiate the peddler story and in 1915, the Fox cottage was moved to Lily Dale, a Spiritualist community near Pomfret in New York State as a permanent exhibit. It was destroyed by fire in September 1955.

The record for the most gruesome poltergeist haunting belongs to the case of the Ashtabula Poltergeist, which took place in Ohio in 1851. A young female medical student awoke one night to find a human corpse she had been dissecting standing beside her bed 'all reeking and ghastly', with its arms folded across its breast. On another night, the woman and her brother saw a human skull dancing about in the moonlight above their beds.

A particularly vindictive poltergeist plagued a Swiss family living in the village of Stans on the shore of Lake Lucerne in the early 1860s. Melchior Joller, a respectable lawyer and member of the Swiss National Council, was so troubled by the appearance of a white figure accompanied by violent knocking noises, inexplicable door locking, voices and the sound of spinning wheels that he fled with his family to Zurich. Joller, a devout Catholic, whose social status was deeply damaged by the haunting, later had a private audience with the Pope, during which he is said to have confided a personal experience with the ghost that he never revealed to anyone else.

☠ ☠ ☠

The Scrapfaggot Green Poltergeist was a wartime sensation that affected the Essex village of Great Leighs in the autumn of 1944. Sheep and horses were found dead in their fields and numerous chickens were drowned in a water butt, haystacks were wrecked, furniture in the village pub was thrown around, the clock in St Mary's church lost an hour each day and the bells played reverse chimes on a Sunday. The happenings, described as being 'partly genuine, partly the work of a practical joker, and partly due to mass-hysteria', were thought to have been started when a large boulder, considered locally to be the gravestone of a seventeenth-century witch, had been knocked over by an American GI in a bulldozer who was widening the roadway for military traffic. When it was repositioned (at the suggestion of ghost hunter Harry Price) the Scrapfaggot Green Poltergeist was heard from no more.

A particularly unusual addition to the poltergeist canon, the case of the Seaford Poltergeist, took place on Long Island, New York, in 1958 and was investigated by Willian Roll and J. Gaither Pratt, two parapsychologists from Duke University in North Carolina. Mr and Mrs Herrmann and their two children, Lucille, aged thirteen, and her twelve-year-old brother Jimmy, lived in an ordinary house on Long Island, New York. For a period of five weeks beginning in early February 1958, they were plagued by the mysterious disturbance and movement of household objects; primarily bottles, the caps of which would fly off by themselves and be found discarded on the floor. Medicine bottles and bottles of shampoo as well as perfume and paint thinners were similarly affected: on several occasions, the popping sounds of the bottle caps were heard by the entire family coming from different rooms in the house when they were all together at the dinner table; at other times, the bottles were discovered with their lids removed and the contents spilling. During one incident, Mr Herrmann and his son were in the bathroom when they observed two bottles move by themselves and fall into the sink. The family became distressed by the happenings and after a report in a local newspaper was seen by Joseph Rhine, the head of the Parapsychology Faculty at Duke, two of his assistants spent over a week at Seaford interviewing witnesses and waiting for phenomena to happen. Pratt and Roll were present when several more bottle-popping incidents took place and also carried out numerous experiments to find a non-ghostly explanation for the disturbances. Despite much experimentation, they were unable to duplicate the effects and came to the conclusion that genuine phenomena were taking place, centred on the young Jimmy Herrmann. On 10 March 1959, the Seaford Poltergeist popped its last bottle, after which the Long Island household returned to normal.

The 1960s was a decade particularly rich in well-authenticated poltergeist cases. In November 1960, eleven-year-old Virginia Campbell who, with her family, had recently left her native Ireland became the focus of the Scottish Sauchie Poltergeist, which was investigated by George Owen who later created 'Philip', the man-made ghost. As well as creating knocking noises and the sound of a bouncing ball in the young girl's bedroom, the poltergeist also followed her to the local primary school, where it made a desk rise into the air and moved a bowl of bulbs across the teacher's desk: the teacher, Margaret Stewart, saw both these incidents and later related them to Dr Owen. The family physician, Dr Nisbet, and a local priest, Revd Lund, both witnessed phenomena and – after setting up a tape recorder and a ciné camera in Virginia's bedroom – succeeded in capturing a variety of strange noises. The girl was also filmed going into a trance and calling out for her friends and her pet dog, which had been left behind in County Donegal.

The tragic case of the Jaboticabal Poltergeist occurred in the south of Brazil in the mid-1960s. The Ferrier family reported being assaulted day and night by a continuous barrage of stones and bricks, which were projected through the windows of their house. The phenomena, which began in December 1965 and lasted several months, appeared to be centred on eleven-year-old Maria Jose Ferrier. Knocks, bangs and raps sounded in her presence, stones flew about and on one occasion her clothes spontaneously ignited, burning a local dentist, Joao Volpe, who had been asked by her frightened parents to examine the girl. Volpe, a follower of Spiritism, a variant of traditional spiritualism practiced and propagated throughout the country by the nineteenth-century French medium, Allan Kardec, was quick to realise that a poltergeist was involved and that he needed expert help. Volpe took Maria to the country's most famous and highly regarded psychic, Chico Xavier (1910–2002), who declared that in a former life the girl had been a witch and was now being tormented by the spirit of one of her restless victims. Xavier allegedly persuaded the tormenting spirit to leave and Maria was returned to her family. However, a short time later, the troubled Maria took her own life by poisoning, apparently believing this to be the only way to stop the paranormal violence. Following her death, the startling phenomena ceased as suddenly as it had begun.

The Black Monk of Pontefract was the name given to a violent poltergeist outbreak that affected a working-class family in the West Riding of Yorkshire between 1966 and 1969. The disturbances were in two separate phases, each centred around one of the two children of Joe and Jean Pritchard. The 'Black Monk' was a tall dark figure that was seen on several occasions inside the house at the height of the haunting and may have been the ghost of a Cluniac monk who, according to local tradition, had been executed for the murder of a woman in the sixteenth century. The first outbreak, which only lasted a few days, seemed to draw its power from fifteen-year-old Philip Pritchard; the second, longer and more violent disturbance was focused on his fourteen-year-old sister Diane. The movement and manipulation of household objects was a major feature of the case. Crockery, family photographs, gloves, painting and decorating equipment, keys and boxes of eggs were all thrown around and animated as though by some form of distinct intelligence; pools of water appeared on the kitchen floor and during one violent attack, Diane Pritchard was dragged up the stairs by her hair. Colin Wilson carried out the most detailed examination of the haunting in the early 1980s and published a lengthy study in his book, *Poltergeist!* (1981).

Another case from the 1960s is the well-known Rosenheim Poltergeist, which occurred in Southern Bavaria and was centred on the offices of a German solicitor named Sigmund Adam. A prominent feature of the disturbances was inexplicable interference with the building's electrical and telephone systems:

lights would mysteriously go out and fuses blew, telephones rang by themselves without any external call coming in and multiple calls were placed to the automated speaking clock, sometimes as many as four in one minute, which was physically impossible to carry out on one of the office handsets in the given time. These strange power surges and telephone calls were confirmed by engineers from both the local electricity board and the telephone company. The German parapsychologist Hans Bender (1907–1991) investigated the case and found that Herr Adam's secretary, nineteen-year-old Annemarie Schaberl, appeared to be the focus of the phenomena: overhead light fittings swung to and fro as she walked along a corridor and the bizarre happenings always commenced and were at their strongest when she was on the premises. Bender and his team succeeded in filming several instances of physical phenomena, including the movement of pictures on the office wall and the swinging lights. Fräulein Schaberl, an unhappy woman who disliked her job and was upset over a recently broken engagement, eventually left the practice, bringing the Rosenheim Poltergeist case to an end.

During the summer of 1979, a lawnmower repair workshop in Cardiff became the playground of 'Pete the Poltergeist', a lively ghost who, as well as throwing stones, made objects appear in people's pockets and caused tools to appear in mid-air and fall to the floor. The case was investigated by the late David Fontana, a highly respected member of the Society for Psychical Research, who like Guy Playfair and Maurice Grosse at Enfield, became convinced that the phenomena was genuine. One witness claimed to have encountered 'Pete' himself, a small boy who he claimed he saw sitting on a beam high up in the workshop roof.

In 1984, Ken Webster, a teacher living in the village of Dodlestone near Chester, made an attempt to communicate with a poltergeist using a home computer. For several weeks, Webster and his nineteen-year-old girlfriend Debbie had been experiencing a series of inexplicable happenings: crockery and cans of food, including tinned cat food, were found stacked into piles around the house; cold breezes sprang up from nowhere when all the windows were closed, and a set of footprints were found on a wall clearly marked out in wet paint. Soon Webster began to notice that his word processor was also being targeted: anomalous words that he knew he had not written began appearing amongst his own scripts. The teacher decided to humour the ghost and began writing out a series of questions which, over a period of time, were answered in an archaic form of English. The poltergeist identified itself as Thomas Harden, and claimed he had lived in the house (and was still living) in the sixteenth century. As the strange conversations continued, it became clear that for the ghost, it was still 1546 and he considered Webster and his girlfriend to be ghosts who were haunting him. Webster checked several of the words written out on the computer with a friend who had majored in Middle English at Oxford and found that many were written in genuine period language. The haunting continued for a number of weeks until Webster found his computer questions going unanswered, after which it was clear that the Dodlestone Poltergeist had left the house for good.

A modern poltergeist haunting from Newcastle is the case of the South Shields Poltergeist. Here, the ghost used modern twentieth-century items to terrify a young family, including writing threats on a child's doodle pad and sending messages which were picked up on a mobile phone. The case was investigated by two local researchers and remains unexplained.

The case of the Carlisle Poltergeist took place over the course of a week in September 2007. Allison Marshall and her family, who lived in the Raffles area of the city, reported a wealth of inexplicable incidents including the movement of objects, sudden temperature drops, raps and knocking sounds, the unsettling sound of a crying baby, as well as the image of a human skull which appeared in the window of a glass cabinet. The haunting was said to have been caused by the ghost of a former neighbour, who departed after a cleansing ceremony was held by a paranormal group from Scotland.

7

HAUNTED BURIAL GROUNDS, WOODS AND BATTLEFIELDS

The annals of organised paranormal investigation reveal that ghostly activity takes place wherever there exists or has existed the presence of man, and the natural world – like the built environment – is a mysterious and haunted realm. After the traditional haunted house, castle or church, cemeteries and similar burial grounds would seem the most natural places for ghosts and phantoms to dwell, and the earth which receives the bodies of the dead, itself imbued with energies and strange forces, also hosts dark woods and forests which have their own ghostly denizens, as well as forming the battlefields on which the sights and sounds of the violent past can on occasion return.

Highgate Cemetery in North London, opened in 1839 and later extended in 1854, is today more associated with stories of vampires than traditional ghosts and hauntings. A once-fashionable and highly regarded Victorian burial ground, known as the final resting place of such notables as John Galsworthy, Sir Charles Cowper and Michael Faraday, by the late 1960s it had deteriorated into an overgrown and decaying ruin, plagued by vandalism, all of which created the ideal conditions in which stories of phantoms and strange happenings flourish. In early 1970, the *Hampstead and Highgate Express* published several accounts of strange figures being seen near the west cemetery gates, which quickly escalated into stories of a modern-day vampire living amongst the tombs. On the night of Friday 13 March 1970, a mass vampire hunt, involving over 100 people, took place and stories of vampires in Highgate were still being published into the 1990s. Ghost stories associated with the East Cemetery, famous for the grave of Karl Marx, include the apparition of a long-haired old woman, said to be a mad lady searching for the graves of her own children that she herself put to death, together with a white-shrouded figure with long bony fingers which drifts in the vicinity of the cemetery gates. In 2005, a local man, Martin Trent, claimed to have encountered the ghost of an old-fashioned-looking man wearing a top hat while walking past the cemetery on his way home.

Leek Cemetery, off the A520 Cheddleton Road in Staffordshire, is haunted by the silent figure of a Victorian-looking man in a tall stovepipe hat and long overcoat. A number of witnesses – including visitors and local residents – have reported seeing the apparition, which remains visible until approached, after which it quickly disappears.

Strange whining and shaking noises and the sound of human voices at one time haunted the superintendent's house at Chingford Mount Cemetery in north-east London. Although some of these phenomena may be put down to subsidence or similar ground water movement, there are also reports of the figure of a man riding a black horse slowly over the cemetery graves.

The graveyard attached to the church of St Nicholas at Canewdon in Essex is traditionally haunted by the ghost of a witch, said to appear headless and dressed in a crinoline, who was executed here during the seventeenth century. The apparition rises from one of the tombs and wanders slowly towards the west gate, where it pauses for a moment before moving quickly down the nearby lanes to the River Crouch, where it vanishes. Anyone unlucky enough to get in her way is lifted up and deposited in the nearest ditch. In 1987, the figure of a woman in a shiny blue dress, possibly one of the De Chanceaux family, former lords of the manor, was seen by a visitor inside the church. She may also haunt the graveyard outside.

The A508 Harborough Road outside Kingsthorpe Cemetery in Northampton is haunted by the apparition of a headless cyclist. In 1940, George Dodds, who had recently moved into the area from Stafford, was walking past the cemetery in heavy snow on his way to the nearby Fox & Hounds pub when he saw the figure of a man on a bicycle suddenly appear in the path of an approaching car. To his horror, Dodds realised there was going to be a collision, but when he reached the spot, both the mysterious man and his machine had completely vanished. The ghost was thought to be that of a local man who had been decapitated in an accident outside the cemetery gates twenty-five years before. Dodds was convinced that the figure he saw had appeared without a head being visible above a muffler round his neck.

THE MADONNA OF BACHELOR'S GROVE

Regarded as one of America's most haunted cemeteries, the abandoned Bachelor's Grove, in Bremen Township, Cook County, Illinois, dates back to the early decades of the nineteenth century; the first burial took place in 1823 and the last interment was carried out in 1965. During the 1970s, visitors to the cemetery began claiming unusual experiences: as well as incidents of interference with cameras and other equipment, strange lights were seen hovering over the neglected graves, as well as a wealth of strange and alarming apparitions which included phantom cars, a spectral farmer complete with horse and ploughshares, and even a phantom house. In August 1991, Dale Kaczmarek, President of the Ghost Research Society, organised a night-time investigation at Bachelor's Grove during the course of which a fellow investigator, Jude Huff-Felz, took a series of photographs using a camera loaded with infrared film. When these were developed, Kaczmarek and his friends were astonished to see the unmistakable figure of a woman with long dark hair wearing an old-fashioned full-length dress sitting on a small chequerboard tombstone in an area known to have been deserted at the time of the investigation. Known today as the Madonna of Bachelor's Grove, thanks to much exposure via the Internet, the image has become one of the most famous modern ghost photographs of the past thirty years.

THE GHOSTLY GUNFIGHTER OF BOOT HILL

Another American cemetery where an intriguing spontaneous ghost photograph was taken in modern times is the famous Boot Hill burying ground in Tombstone, Arizona, whose 300 or so occupants include three men killed during the famous 'Gunfight at the OK Corral' on 26 October 1881. In 1996, Terry Clanton, a descendent of the famous outlaw, Joseph 'Ike' Clanton, visited the cemetery with a friend in order to have publicity photographs taken in 1880s period costume. Following the photo shoot, Clanton took the roll of film to a local drug store and waited while the photographs were developed. Neither of the two men were prepared for what they found when looking through the pictures a short while later: in one photograph, the clear image of a man wearing a black hat and light-coloured shirt and carrying what appears to be a long-bladed knife was visible from the waist upwards amongst the gravestones behind where Clanton's friend was posing in the cemetery. Both men were adamant that the photograph was not a hoax and that they were alone in that particular part of Boot Hill when the picture was taken.

THE MYSTERY OF RESURRECTION MARY

One of America's most famous phantom hitchhiker stories is centred around the Resurrection Cemetery on Archer Avenue, Justice, Illinois, 12 miles south-west of Chicago city centre.

Sightings of a blonde female figure wearing a white dress that vanishes in mysterious circumstances have been reported with some regularity back as far as the 1930s. According to tradition, the ghost is that of a young hit-and-run victim who was knocked down and killed outside the cemetery gates after attending a dance at the local Oh Henry Ballroom, today known as the Willowbrook. Two possible contenders for Mary's ghost are Anna Norkus, who was killed in a car accident while returning from the ballroom in 1927, and Mary Bregovy, who also died in a car crash in 1934; both women are buried in the cemetery.

☠ ☠ ☠

The apparition of a six-year-old Victorian boy haunts the old cemetery of St John's in the village of Hopwas near Tamworth in Staffordshire. In 1982, work by members of the village Women's Institute to catalogue the various graves uncovered the burial site of a young boy who had died locally on 15 March 1878. Not long after, there were three separate incidents of the sighting of a small figure in the immediate vicinity of the same grave. Interestingly, despite adults being present on all these occasions, the ghostly boy was only visible to the children present, one of whom was the same age as the child on the gravestone.

As well as the haunted cemetery, Hopwas Wood – on the north side of the village adjacent to the A51 Hopwas Hill – has a similar haunted reputation as well as associations with local witchcraft. In 1984, a local coven from the Tamworth area were arrested during a night-time raid by police and there are persistent reports of walkers and visitors encountering a strangely tall figure, dressed in the manner of a priest or cleric, which quickly vanishes when approached. Strange lights have also been seen among the trees. In December 2010, the mystery surrounding the area deepened when members of the West Midlands Ghost Club uncovered a curious rectangular tablet, made of copper and engraved with a star-shaped symbol and strange writing within the wood. A short time before, a local man, Andrew Lee, claimed he had found a strange Egyptian-like clay statue in the same area while out walking his father's dog. The origins of these finds and their possible connections with ghostly activity reported in the area remain a mystery.

Another wood with both occult and paranormal connections is Badgerdell Wood, also known as the Bluebell Wood, on the outskirts of Caddington, near Luton in Bedfordshire. In April 1963, police and RSPCA inspector, John Goodenough, uncovered the severed heads of six cows and a horse, which appeared to have been used as part of a Satanic ceremony, possibly linked with the desecration of an abandoned church at nearby Clophill the previous month. In 1979, a group of Luton schoolchildren claimed to have encountered a bizarre 'owlman' apparition, which pursued them out of the wood and through a tunnel under the nearby M1 motorway. A report of a black dog haunting has also been collected from the same area.

Like Badgerdell Wood, Clapham Wood on the South Downs, 3¾ miles north-west of Worthing in West Sussex, is another location which garnered a sinister and haunted reputation during the 1970s. Charles Walker, a local investigator, together with journalist Toyne Newton, reported a growing catalogue of mysterious activity in and around the wood including strangely-shaped footprints; an eerie black mass seen amongst the trees; a powerful debilitating force which on occasion appeared to temporarily take control of animals and people walking in a tree-lined grove known as The Chestnuts; and the regular disappearances of domestic animals, including several dogs and a horse, as well as the appearance of strange lights and shapes in the night sky.

The woods surrounding Robin Hood's Grave, a Victorian memorial in the grounds of the Kirklees Park Estate in West

Yorkshire, are haunted by the apparition of a woman in a long white dress with long sleeves, thought by some to be the wicked prioress of Kirklees Priory, who tricked folk hero Robin Hood and bled him to death. A local musician, Roger Williams, claimed to have seen the ghost on two occasions; the first time in 1963 and again in 1972. Both times she appeared with mad staring eyes and exuded an aura of malice and rage.

The former Windsor Forest, today known as Windsor Great Park and for many years the private hunting ground of Windsor Castle, is traditionally haunted by Herne the Hunter, a mysterious nature spirit usually represented as appearing wrapped in chains with antlers growing out of his head and riding a phantom black horse, surrounded by a pack of baying ghost dogs. The first mention of Herne in literature is by William Shakespeare in his play *The Merry Wives of Windsor*, first published in 1602. He is also associated with the Wild Hunt, a ghostly procession of dead

huntsmen, horses and hounds, which is reported from several countries and has its origins in Teutonic and Norse mythology. Whatever his origins, Herne the Hunter, or at least a ghostly horseman described as such, has been seen with some regularity down through the centuries. Henry VIII claimed he saw the ghost while out riding and there were half a dozen sightings during the twentieth century alone, including one by a Coldstream guardsman and another by a servant at Windsor Castle. During the reign of Richard II, one of the royal huntsmen hanged himself from an oak tree (known as Herne's Oak), which survived until it was destroyed during a storm in 1863. A replacement tree was later planted by Queen Victoria. A ghostly figure has also been seen in the vicinity of another ancient tree known as William the Conqueror's Oak, which stands opposite the park's Cranborne Gate.

One of the most remarkable and disturbing cases of an encounter with a haunting apparition is that claimed by the English ghost hunter, Robert Thurston Hopkins (1884–1958). In his book, *Adventures with Phantoms*, published in 1946, Thurston Hopkins described an incident that allegedly took place during a midnight ghost walk in the 1930s in Glydwish Wood, a wild and overgrown location with a sinister reputation on the South Downs in East Sussex. After leading a party of thirty walkers across the countryside around Burwash village, Hopkins took his group around the edge of the wood while a journalist friend, given the name Blunden in the book, explored inside by himself. After some time, the main group heard a distressing cry and Blunden was eventually discovered wandering in a distressed and confused state amongst the trees: he later claimed to have encountered the apparition of a dead man with rotting skin and a distended neck, as if from a hangman's rope, which had blundered out of the undergrowth towards him. A month later, the ghost hunter returned to Glydwish Wood accompanied by an assistant and on this occasion encountered the frightening figure for himself, 'a ragged man, choking and clutching at its long scraggy neck, his eyes bulging out of a withered and almost fleshless face'. Thurston Hopkins was of the opinion that the ghost was that of Daniel Leney, a local thief who had been hanged in 1827 for the murder of a farmer named Benjamin Russell.

💀 💀 💀

In the early autumn of 1914, the advance of German troops into France was temporarily arrested by a military engagement known as the Battle of Mons. On 23 August, a British Expeditionary Force comprising cavalry and two infantry divisions totalling 80,000 men held the vastly superior German First Army of around 160,000 soldiers at Mons in Belgium for several hours before staging a tactical withdrawal. The British suffered over 1,600 casualties, while the opposing First Army lost over three times that amount of men. During the following months and well into the following year, stories began circulating both at home and among the Allied troops of the appearance of an army of phantom soldiers, which had attacked the German soldiers and protected the British Army as it retreated. Described variously as a company of ghostly bowmen from Agincourt, a mysterious luminous cloud, and most famously as angelic warriors, the so-called 'Angels of Mons', the story gained much exposure and popularity, both during the Great War and in the years that followed. Despite many people at the time wanting to believe in the existence of the angels, the story was in fact a hoax created by the Welsh writer Arthur Machen (1863–1947) who, just days after the battle, wrote a short story titled 'The Bowmen' which described an account of ghostly soldiers protecting a platoon of British soldiers. The story was published in the *London Evening News* and was quickly accepted as fact. Machen later issued the story as a separate book with an explanatory note as to its origins, but despite this, the story continued to be considered as a document of real events for many years.

If the ghosts of Mons can be dismissed as a journalistic invention, there are other battlefields and places of violent conflict where tales of hauntings are less easy to explain away. At Halidon Hill on the outskirts of Berwick-upon-Tweed in Northumberland, where the soldiers of Edward III fought and defeated the Scots on 19 July 1333, the aural haunting of a phantom battle along with the appearance of a ghostly soldier have been reported on several occasions, including the shouts and exhortations of fighting men, the ring of steel and screams and moans of the wounded and the dying.

Phenomena associated with haunted battlefields, as at Halidon Hill, often comprises a ghostly soundtrack of their violent past, and as such are closely linked with aural timeslip hauntings such as the Dieppe Raid case mentioned earlier (*see* Chapter 1). On the site of the Battle of Naseby, which took place in Northamptonshire on 14 June 1645, similar cyclical sounds of paranormal conflict have been reported, often in the month of June, while in Somerset at Westonzoyland on the outskirts of Bridgewater, the sound of gunfire accompanied by pounding hooves, drumming and the shouts and cries of human voices is thought to be a psychic replay of the Battle of Sedgemoor, the final engagement of the ill-fated West Country Rebellion, which took place on 6 July 1685.

Not all battlefield ghosts, however, are invisible soundtracks. One winter's night in 1950, Miss E. Smith was walking through the open countryside near Dunnichen in Angus, Scotland, when she became aware of what appeared to be flickering lights a short way off amongst the moorland. As she came closer, she observed several figures in curiously ancient-looking clothing moving about in the darkness as though a search was taking place by torchlight. The vision lasted for several minutes before gradually fading away. It seems likely that this was a psychic window on the aftermath of the Battle of Nechtansmere, which took place in AD 685 between the Picts and the Northumbrian soldiers of King Ecgfirth, when the conquering Picts were searching the bodies of the dead and dying.

8

HAUNTED PUBS, TAVERNS AND INNS

Public houses and inns have been traditional meeting places providing shelter and company – as well as staging posts for travellers – for centuries, so it is no surprise that these buildings and their environs are some of the most commonly haunted in the country. Here are just a few of the many haunted hostelries from around Britain.

The Bingley Arms in the picturesque Yorkshire village of Bardsey is considered to be the oldest inn in England, with a known history dating back to at least AD 953. Its ghosts include a phantom dog as well as the apparitions of a young woman and a spectral cavalier.

The ghost of Emily Brontë (1818–1848), the author of *Wuthering Heights*, has long been associated with The Weavers pub and restaurant (formerly the Toby Jugg) on West Street, Haworth, in the West Riding of Yorkshire. She was first seen by the then owner, Keith Ackroyd, in 1966; he described the phantom novelist as a smiling and giggling figure which appeared out of a bluish-grey haze wearing a bonnet and long dress with a basket on her arm. The ghost, which has also been seen in a doorway of the nearby Black Bull Inn as well as near a waterfall on the path leading to the ruined Top Withens farmhouse (the inspiration for Wuthering Heights itself) is said to appear once a year on 19 December, the anniversary of Brontë's death.

The Bluebell Inn at Belmesthorpe in Rutland, believed to have been built on the site of a former monastery, was for many years haunted by the apparition of a hunchback as well as the smell of incense, which often filled the building during the period of the full moon.

An instance of a ghost seemingly taking a bath was reported in 1971 from a public house in Bridge of Earn, Perthshire. The then landlord, Mr Young, went to the bathroom upstairs but found the door locked and the sound of splashing water coming from inside. Going back a few minutes later, he discovered the bathroom door wide open and the bath, all the towels and linen completely dry. The building is also known to be haunted by the sounds of footsteps and strange crying noises, which have been heard in one of the upper corridors.

The George, a former eighteenth-century coaching inn on the High Street in the village of Silsoe in Bedfordshire, is haunted by the apparition of a woman in grey, said to be Lady Elisabeth Grey of nearby Wrest Park. The haunting dates back to at least 1945, when a barmaid saw a figure in the roadway outside. In 1960, a workman moving beer kegs in the yard looked up and saw a grey form wearing a large picture hat pass close by which disappeared from view through a doorway. The George is also said to be haunted by the spirit of an angry man, which was photographed by members of the Anglia Paranormal Investigation Society during a visit in October 2013.

Another George – the George Hotel in Market Street, Hatherleigh, in Devon – is said to be haunted by the apparition of a naked woman.

THE HAUNTED PUBS OF LONDON

The ghostly history of the capital was first chronicled by Peter Underwood in 1973, and since then several other authors and ghost hunters including Richard Jones, Neil Arnold, David Brandon and Richard Felix have added to the records with a growing library of books and video documentaries. Many of London's hostelries and pubs have supernatural associations that befit their presence in one of the most famous and haunted cities in the world.

Ye Olde Gate House pub in Highgate Village, North London, is traditionally haunted by the ghost of Mother Marnes, a widow who was murdered during a robbery on the premises many years ago. As well as her black-robed apparition, a former landlord claimed to have seen her ghostly cat, which was apparently killed with her. In October 1966, Highgate resident Tony Abbott, who had spent an evening in the Gate House listening to a jazz band, encountered a tall figure wearing what he later described as a Guy Fawkes-type hat and a long dark cloak in one of the ground-floor corridors. The person disappeared through a closed door and Abbott also reported hearing a strange rushing sound and feeling an inexplicable sensation of coldness and panic in its immediate vicinity. Local husband and wife researchers David and Della Farrant have established that a ley line connects Ye Olde Gate House with several nearby landmarks, including the Circle of Lebanon tombs in Highgate Cemetery, St Michael's church, a former nunnery now occupied by the Hillcrest council estate, and the site of an ancient Roman settlement in Highgate Woods.

Now closely associated with the famous and unsolved serial murders of Jack the Ripper, two of whose victims are said to have drunk there before their deaths in the autumn of 1888, the Ten Bells pub on the corner of Commercial Street and Fournier Street in London's Spitalfields is also a haunted building. In recent years, live-in staff have reported the sounds of footsteps and laughter when alone on the premises, as well as the appearance of a male figure, described as being an elderly man in Victorian-style clothing, who is thought to be a former tenant landlord.

For several years in the 1960s, the former Horn Inn along Crucifix Lane in Bermondsey was haunted by the unsettling sound of a crying child. The Wrights, who held the tenancy until 1970, claimed that the noises were heard by a number of different people including, on one occasion, by two people simultaneously. They estimated that the voice was that of a child around eight or nine-years-old and also reported minor poltergeist activity in the building. Following a visit by a medium, during which a 'rescue circle' was held for the haunting 'entity', the phenomena ceased. The pub, which later changed its name to the Czar Bar, is currently operated as the Suchards Bar and Thai Restaurant.

Formerly an officers' mess for the Duke of Wellington's Regiment at the time of Waterloo, The Guardsman, now long known by its present name of The Grenadier in Wilton Row, Belgravia, is one of London's most familiar haunted sites. A cyclical haunting occurs here during the month of September and is said to have its origins in the death of one of Wellington's officers, beaten to death on the steps leading down to what is now the beer cellar after being caught cheating at cards by a group of his fellow soldiers. The haunting was first investigated by Peter Underwood, at the time President of the Ghost Club, who interviewed several witnesses, including members of the Grigg family who held the licence in the 1960s. He also visited on one occasion with clairvoyant Trixie Allingham, who picked up residual impressions of the dying guardsman's final moments. The ghost has been described as a shadowy figure, seen hovering

in one of the bedrooms, as well as a more substantial male s
which appears walking up the main staircase before vanishing
suddenly. Successive landlords have also reported unusual
happenings, particularly physical phenomena, such as the
movement of objects and interference with lights and water taps
during the night.

The Mitre in Craven Terrace, Lancaster Gate, is haunted by
the ghost of a Jacobean scullery maid named Mary, who came
to London seeking work. Unfortunately for Mary, an affair
with the youthful Lord Craven ended in her untimely death
when she was stabbed to death by the aristocrat's wife in the old
servants' quarters, a part of the building now used as a private
restaurant. The sound of a crying woman, said to be an echo of
the unhappy Mary, has been reported on the premises for many
years. Staff have also reported encountering an unseen presence
and experiencing psychic touches and sensations of being pushed
and manhandled on the stairs between the main bar and the
Scullery restaurant. The Mitre also boasts another ghost: that of
a Victorian coachman, seen in the basement area at the rear of
the building which backs on to Lancaster Mews.

In 1854, a London physician, Dr John Snow, prevented
the spread of a cholera outbreak by identifying a water pump
in present day Broadwick Street, Soho, as the source of the
infection. The site of the pump is marked by a memorial and,
befitting its famous association, the Victorian public house at the
junction of Lexington Street a short distance away is haunted
by the apparition of a sinister-looking man, possibly a cholera
victim, who has been glimpsed on a number of occasions in the
bar area, his face distorted as if in great pain.

The former sites of gallows and gibbeting posts have
given many locations around the country eerie and haunted
reputations. The Thomas à Becket, once a landmark public
house but now used as an art gallery on the Old Kent Road in
Bermondsey, is one such building. A gallows is known to have

.ighteenth century and perhaps some of the
an emotion associated with this time has left
ons on the psychic fabric of this particular part
the hostelry that was subsequently built on the
ant landlords and former owners claimed to have
expe.. .range happenings on the premises down through
the years, the most unusual occurrence being the appearance
of quantities of coal in the nature of a paranormal apport,
which would be found in the unused open grates, as though the
fireplaces had been made up ready for lighting. A room at the top
of the building was regarded as being the most haunted part of
the establishment: animals avoided it and showed distinct signs of
distress if taken inside, and humans alike regarded it with unease
and seldom stayed there for long. Like a number of public houses
across the country, the first floor of The Thomas à Becket was
used for many years as a gymnasium, giving rise to its familiar
alternate title of the 'Boxers' Pub': heavyweight champion Henry
Cooper trained here during the 1950s and early '60s, while
another boxer, Joe Lucy, claimed that he had heard ghostly
voices and the sound of whispering while training for the British

Welterweight Championship here
in 1956.

The ghost of highwayman Dick
Turpin, hanged in 1739 for the capital
offence of horse theft, is one of the
busiest phantoms in Britain, being
associated with many landmarks,
public houses and buildings across
the country between London and
York, where he ultimately met his
end. Turpin is said to be the shadowy
figure seen in the roadway outside
the well-known Spaniards Inn,
a sixteenth-century tollgate inn on

the edge of Hampstead Heath. Ghostly hoofbeats heard nearby are considered to be those of the highwayman's famous mount, Black Bess, while the apparition of a woman in a white dress is said to haunt the beer garden at night. The Spaniards' other association with the supernatural is a fictional one, being the place where Professor Van Helsing and his fellow vampire hunters enjoyed a hearty meal before setting out to stake and destroy the tragic Lucy Westenra in *Dracula*.

🦇 🦇 🦇

The ghost of a serving maid known as Geranium Jane at one time haunted the former King's Head Hotel in Cuckfield, West Sussex. According to tradition, Jane was murdered by her employer in the nineteenth century after she became pregnant and, unwanted by her lover, was silenced forever after being struck on the head with a plant pot. Jane's ghost was said to be most active when couples involved in illicit relationships and extra-marital affairs were staying at the King's Head, shaking the beds as a sign of disapproval and turning the atmosphere of the room icy cold. On rare occasions Jane herself put in an appearance: a tragic figure, seen pacing around inside the building with blood streaming down her face.

The ghost at The Bell Inn at Studham in Bedfordshire had a fetish for brushes and yellow dusters. In 1965, the licensee Jim Kevan and his wife reported numerous items disappearing without trace. On one occasion, Mr Kevan tried to tempt the ghost by leaving a bottle of gin with the dusters in the kitchen, but these were two spirits that didn't mix and only the usual items were taken. The ghost was thought to be that of an old woman who had lived in the building many years before.

The ghost of Suki, an attractive sixteen-year-old barmaid from the late eighteenth century, haunts the George and Dragon pub in West Wycombe in Buckinghamshire. In 1967, an American tourist staying in one of the upstairs rooms reported the sensation of being touched by icy hands as well as witnessing the appearance of a strangely illuminated figure which vanished as soon as he switched on the lights. Suki, who – according to legend – was attacked by three local youths in the nearby Hellfire Caves and died in the George the following day wearing a beautiful white dress, is thought to be the figure seen looking out of the upper windows as well as the woman with a 'sad, lost expression' encountered by the landlady sitting beside one of the fireplaces in the early 1990s. The apparition remained visible for some moments before quickly fading away.

One of England's most haunted pubs, the sixteenth-century White Hart Hotel in Holywell Hill, St Albans, was originally known as the Hartshorn and its oldest sections date back to around 1500. In 1746, Simon Fraser, 11th Lord Lovat and the last man to be beheaded in Britain, stayed a night here on his way to the Tower of London. In 1820, a woman named Elizabeth Wilson, who was riding on the roof of the Northampton stagecoach, was killed when she struck her head on the archway leading into the stable yard. There is a possibility that she may be one of several ghosts seen and felt here by staff and guests over the years. As well as the figure of a woman, the apparition of a small girl has been seen standing by the fireplace in the main bar room as well as in a room upstairs. Cold breezes, the poltergeist-like movement of objects and an invisible presence have been experienced as well as ghostly writing, said to have appeared on a bedroom mirror.

One warm summer night in the mid-1970s, Detective Constable Roger Ryder was driving along the A456 dual carriageway between Halesowen and Hagley in Worcestershire. As he approached The Gypsy's Tent public house (today renamed as The Badger's Set), Ryder noticed that the windows of the building appeared to be glowing, despite the fact that it was past midnight, long after the premises should have been closed.

Suddenly, the figure of a man dressed in the style of a cavalier, in red clothing complete with a wide-brimmed hat, high leather boots and a sword, appeared to run from the car park at the front of the building and out into the roadway, on a collision course with the policeman's car. Horrified, Ryder found himself approaching the man – who was now standing directly in the road in front of him – at around 60mph. Despite jamming on the brakes, he was unable to prevent the car from striking the figure and, desperately trying to control the careering vehicle, ended up facing the wrong way further down the road. Certain that he had killed a drunken reveller from a fancy dress party, Ryder got out and ran back to the spot, but the figure had completely vanished. The windows of the pub were also in darkness. The ghostly cavalier's origin may lie in a violent skirmish that took place in nearby Foxcote Lane during the English Civil War.

9

PHANTOM ANIMALS

hostly animals form an interesting subdivision of apparitional hauntings. Surprisingly, man's best friend, the dog, is not the most commonly reported, but there are accounts of many different type of ghostly creature, several interesting accounts of which are included here.

In the 1870s, a phantom white rabbit was often seen with such regularity 'cavorting' in the churchyard of St Mary's in the Baum in Rochdale, Lancashire that a local poet composed a poem castigating the creature for the trouble and fright it caused local people passing by the church at night. The rabbit's paranormal nature was seemingly confirmed at the time by its imperviousness to buckshot, as a number of travellers reported taking pot shots at the creature, but it should be no surprise that the animal has not been reported from the area now for over a century. Incidentally, in the 1970s, the apparition of a man was also seen drifting out of the same churchyard and across into a neighbouring market place where it disappeared into a particular corner.

The lanes around the village of Burnham Green, near Welwyn Garden City in Hertfordshire, are traditionally haunted by the apparition of several ghostly white horses, which are both riderless and headless. The White Horse pub at nearby Datchworth is said to take its name from a horse from Welches Farm, which was killed along with its owner, a Royalist sympathiser, by Cromwell's men during the Civil War. Both were beheaded and their heads left side by side on spikes as a warning to others.

The stretch of the A30 road at Windwhistle Hill between Chard and Crewkerne on the Devon and Dorset border is haunted by the ghostly hoof-beats of a galloping horse, said to be the psychic residue of a bloody encounter between a hapless smuggler and customs men during the reign of George III. Accounts of the phenomenon were being reported as late as the 1970s.

THE BLACK HOUNDS OF DEATH

'Black Shuck' is the collective name given to large phantom dogs, which are known to both ghost hunters and folklorists alike. There are many derivatives, some of which are associated with the sites of former gibbets and gallows, and they go by a number of striking and colourful local names.

The North of England is known as the hunting ground of 'Padfoot', an animal the size of a donkey whose feet are turned backwards. In Lancashire, a similar beast is called by a number of names including 'Trash', 'Striker' and the 'Boggart' which, when seen, utters a terrible screeching sound before sinking down into the ground and disappearing. In Northumberland and parts of Yorkshire, the 'Barguest' is described as being a large black dog with blazing eyes, while 'Shuck' or 'Shag' haunts the cemeteries and graveyards of East Anglia on dark stormy nights, terrifying wayward travellers unlucky enough to cross its path with its single flaming eye. The legend of the Black Dog ghost is strongest in the West Country, where it is known as the 'Yeth Hound' and occurs at a number of locations, including Uplyme in Devon and the Blackmoor Gate crossroads on Exmoor.

One phantom hound that breaks the Black Dog tradition is the Scottish 'Lamper', which haunts the wilds of the Hebrides Islands and whose appearance is considered to be an omen of approaching death. This ghostly dog is said to be white rather than the traditional black and to have no visible tail.

The 'Hell Hound of Luton' haunts the slopes of Galley Hill to the north-east of the town, where witches were once hung and left to rot in iron gibbets. According to traditional accounts, one stormy night in the early eighteenth century, a thunderbolt struck one of the gibbet posts and set the tar-soaked corpses alight. The bodies and gibbet burned so fiercely that it appeared to observers watching in the villages below that the entire hill was on fire. Amongst the flames, what appeared to be a large black dog was seen leaping and dancing until both gibbet and corpses were reduced to ashes, at which point the phantom hound gave a terrible howl and vanished down into the smoking ground. A sighting of the ghost dog today is considered an omen of impending disaster.

On 24 August 1751, Thomas Colley, a chimney sweep from Tring in Hertfordshire, was hanged for the murder of Ruth Osborne, a local villager who, along with her husband John, many believed practised witchcraft. Colley had led a mob that, in April of the same year, had dragged the couple from a nearby workhouse and subjected them to the 'swimming' ordeal in the village pond at nearby Wilstone, where Ruth died after she was pushed down into the water with a stick. Colley was hanged at Gubblecote Cross and the area is today reputed to be haunted by his ghost, which returns in the form of a large black dog with burning eyes.

Conflicting reports surround the Black Dog of Leeds Castle, an unusual canine haunting from the time that the Wykeham-Martin family were in residence in the years before the First World War. Some accounts credit the sudden appearance of a phantom black retriever inside the castle apartments as an omen of impending death and ill fortune for those unlucky enough to see or experience it. However, ghost hunter James Wentworth Day collected a first-hand account (later published by Peter Underwood in his book *This Haunted Isle*) of an incident when the ghost dog actually saved a life rather than cursed it. On this occasion, a member of the Wykeham-Martin family was sewing in a window seat in one of the bay windows overlooking the castle moat when she saw a large black dog walk across the room and abruptly vanish into the wall opposite. Seconds after the lady got up and crossed the room to examine the spot where the spectral animal had disappeared, the ancient bay window where she had been sitting suffered a massive structural failure and the entire window crashed down into the moat below.

Hergest Court, a stone and timbered building on the outskirts of the market town of Kington, is the originator of a number of Herefordshire Black Dog hauntings. In 1959, a tenant farmer named Jack Morris woke one night to see a large black dog-like apparition crouched beside his bed. He described the animal as red-eyed with wicked-looking fangs and also claimed to have seen the same dog several times around the farm. This particular Black Dog is traditionally believed to be the unquiet spirit of Thomas Vaughan, a tyrannical former owner who died at the Battle of Banbury during the Wars of the Roses in 1469. Known as 'Black Vaughan', he and his equally villainous wife, Gethen, were feared by the local populace for their ungodly behaviour and all breathed a sigh of relief when Thomas was laid to rest in St Mary's churchyard. Unfortunately, the former lord of the manor's influence continued to reach out from beyond the grave: Vaughan's ghost, sometimes appearing as a fearsome black bull, and at other instances as a fearsome apparition with demonic eyes, rendered travellers abroad at night insane with terror and caused other acts of local mischief, including damage to livestock and the wrecking of farm carts. Tradition holds that Vaughan's spirit was finally exorcised and imprisoned in a snuffbox, which was thrown into a pond in the grounds of Hergest Court for good measure. Despite this, strange happenings in the area are still associated with the legend of 'Black Vaughan'. In 1974, a couple passing by St Mary's churchyard at night claimed to have seen a legless creature surrounded by a strange pink glow that drifted across the road in front of their car before vanishing into the front of the vicarage. In 1981, another ghostly animal, this time quite discernible as a black dog, was seen sitting in the road by Irene Cole and her husband, who were driving into Kington on the approach close to a rounded hill known as the Stanner Rocks. The Coles' car appeared to strike the animal, which abruptly disappeared. Despite a search of the area, no trace of the dog, which had appeared solid and lifelike, was found.

Not all Black Dog ghosts haunt in lonely roads and isolated churchyards. The former Newgate Prison in the City of London was said to have been haunted by the apparition of a black hound, which appeared regularly over many years prior to an execution. The dog was first reported some time towards the end

of the sixteenth century and has its origins in the case of an inmate on remand, who was cannibalised by his fellow prisoners before standing trial. Several other ghosts reported from Newgate, which was demolished at the beginning of the twentieth century and on the site of which the Old Bailey court now stands, include the limping figure of a hanged man, heard and seen on the Dead Man's Walk where executed criminals were buried, as well as the apparitions of Victorian baby farmer, Amelia Dyer, and the forger, Henry Fauntleroy.

🐱 🐱 🐱

In the late 1960s, Killakee House on the outskirts of Dublin developed the reputation of being one of Ireland's most haunted buildings. As well as strange noises, poltergeist activity and several unidentified apparitions including a nun and a tall Eurasian man, the house's owners, Margaret and Nicholas O'Brien, reported the appearance of a frightening phantom cat 'the size of a biggish dog, with terrible eyes', which was seen by a number of people in the grounds and on one occasions sitting crouched in the hallway near the open front door. In the summer of 1969 and again in July 1970, exorcisms were carried out at Killakee, which helped to lessen the haunting. After a deformed human skeleton, unearthed by builders digging up the kitchen floor to lay pipework, was given a religious reinterment, the ghostly activity in and around the house ceased.

On 9 July 1904, the novelist H. Rider Haggard suffered a distressing nightmare that disturbed his wife to the point that she shook him awake. Haggard described seeing a vision of a black retriever dog named Bob which belonged to one of his daughters lying fatally injured in undergrowth beside a stretch of water; the animal's neck seemed to be broken and Haggard had the impression that it was letting him know it was dying. The following morning, the dog, which had been seen in the house the previous day, was found to be missing and was discovered four days later floating dead in a nearby river. It had been struck by a train on the night Haggard had had his nightmare.

Amongst the many curious incidents reported from in and around the site of Borley Rectory down through the years is the incident of the 'strange insect' which took place on the afternoon of 22 August 1938 when Mrs Margaret Wilson visited the house to paint a picture in the garden. As she sat at her easel close to the large summerhouse where Revd Harry Bull had spent many hours ghost watching in the years before the First World War, Mrs Wilson was disturbed by the appearance of a bizarre flying insect which she later described to psychic investigator Harry Price as being around 3in long, black in colour and with large goggle-eyes like bloomy black grapes. Neither the artist or the ghost hunter were able to identify the species with any certainty, and Price later wrote that it was just one of the many 'impossible' things that have happened in this '"enchanted" Rectory'.

The ruins of Lydford Castle, a medieval prison on the north-western outskirts of Dartmoor, were at one time reputed to be haunted by the apparition of a phantom black pig.

The beast was thought to be the earthbound spirit of the brutal Sir Richard Grenville, the Royalist commander who was in charge of a military prison here during the Civil War.

Another bovine haunting is the bizarre case of the Screaming Pigs of Uphill. Near to the small Buckinghamshire village of St Leonards in the Chiltern Hills, the grunts, screams and roars of a mass of mysterious phantom animals have been heard on cloudy moonless nights. When glimpsed, these ghostly beasts have been described as appearing like a herd of black pigs that paw at the ground as well as gore and bite at one another. At one time, local belief credited the haunting's origins to the siting of a gibbet on the road between St Leonards and nearby Cholesbury, but there is no evidence for a gallows at this spot and the origins of these strange ghosts remain a mystery.

POLTERGEIST ANIMALS

Strange phantom animals and animal-like apparitions have been a feature of a number of poltergeist hauntings down through the years.

In the case of the Bell Witch, the catalyst seemed to be the appearance of several unidentified creatures, one like a dog, and the other similar to a turkey, which vanished when farmer John Bell fired his shotgun at them.

The Sandfeldt Poltergeist took place in Germany in 1722 in the home of farmer Hans Joachim Dunckelman. The farmer's children claimed to see many frightening apparitions, which appeared like unknown species of animal. The first ghosts appeared on 12 February 1722 and were likened to a plague of mysterious cats that ran about inside the house. They were accompanied by a ghostly dog with short ears. A few days later the children were playing in the attic when they were startled by another phantom dog, yellow in colour with a cow's snout and only three legs. The following month, the same children claimed to see the ghost of a swineherd with a whip driving a group of small calf-like animals out of a shed on the farm.

The haunting of Willington Mill on Tyneside took place in the first half of the nineteenth century. The home of the Procter family was plagued by an onslaught of sinister and inexplicable phenomena, which included the sound of voices and heavy footsteps, raps, knocks and rustling noises, bell-ringing, the appearance of disembodied heads and faces, and coughing, moaning and tapping sounds. Several people claimed to see a strange white creature, like a large cat with a long snout, which walked through closed doors and disappeared. On one occasion it was seen by Joseph Procter walking straight into the open furnace door. The Procter children also reported the appearance of a phantom monkey, which appeared from nowhere and jumped across the nursery floor, pulling at their bootstraps and tickling their feet.

Two poltergeist animals made an appearance during the haunting of Epworth rectory in 1717. One was a badger-like animal seen scurrying under the beds by the Wesley children, while several servants claimed they had observed the head of a strange rodent peering out at them from a crack near the kitchen fireplace.

🐾 🐾 🐾

The grounds of Wilbury House, a Grade I listed building at Newton Tony in Wiltshire, are haunted by the ghost of a friendly dog. Visitors have reported being accompanied along the drive by a retriever, which disappears suddenly when they reach the house.

A royal ghost dog haunts the garden of Barton Manor at East Cowes on the Isle of Wight. Formerly an Augustinian Oratory, the house was bought by Queen Victoria in 1845 as an annexe to Osborne House and it was here that one of the queen's favourite collie dogs drowned in a skating lake built in the grounds by Prince Albert. It was seen in the 1940s by a Miss Holt, who ran an antiquarian bookshop on the island. She described seeing a small dog which she took to be real until it gradually faded away in front of her.

An affectionate but slightly annoying ghost dog is the spectral King Charles spaniel which has been seen in daylight running and yapping along the outside terrace at Ham House near Petersham in south-west London. The animal has also been observed by staff wandering around inside the house but the origins of this particular haunting are unknown.

Athelhampton Hall, a fifteenth-century house built for the Martyn family near Puddletown in Dorset, is haunted by the spectre of a tame monkey which was left to starve to death when its owner committed suicide. The ghost was seen on several occasions on a hidden staircase leading from the Great Chamber up into the Long Gallery, and the monkey seems also to be represented in the eerie motto attached to the Martyn family crest: 'He who looks at Martyn's ape, Martyn's ape shall look at him.'

The Ghostly Catch, a huge shoal of phantom fish, is said to appear during raging storms offshore from Drumnacrogha or the Castle of the Scald at Killilog, County Sligo in Ireland. The fish have been reported on a number of occasions, by local fisherman as well as Captain Don Francesco de Cuellar, a survivor of the Spanish Armada who was shipwrecked off the coast at Sligo in 1588.

As well as vampires, fashionable Highgate in North London is also famous for perhaps the capital's most bizarre haunting, the Phantom Chicken of Pond Square. On 9 April 1626, the English scientist and philosopher, Sir Francis Bacon, died in Highgate at the home of his friend, Lord Arundel. Bacon had contracted pneumonia after leaving his open carriage on a freezing night a few days before to carry out an impromptu experiment in refrigeration while being driven in the company of the royal physician, Dr Witherborne. Noticing that grass buried under fallen snow still appeared fresh when uncovered by the carriage's wheels, Sir Francis had instructed his coachman to buy a fresh chicken from a poulterer's shop on Highgate Hill and, after plucking it in the middle of Pond Square, proceeded to stuff it with frozen snow, producing not only the world's first frozen chicken, but (according to local history) a ghostly fowl into the bargain. Reports of the sighting of a featherless spectral bird in the immediate area of Pond Square seem to have begun soon after Bacon's death and continued with some infrequency up until the late 1960s. There were a number of encounters during the Second World War when, among others, a local family, an ARP Warden, and a serviceman home on leave all claimed to have seen and heard the ghost hopping and squawking about in the darkness and proving its paranormality by disappearing through solid objects. The last reported sightings date from 1969 when a stranded motorist saw the phantom bird, and a year later, when it disturbed a courting couple in the doorway of a nearby house.

One night in January 1816, a sentry on guard outside the Martin Tower at the Tower of London had a strange and unnerving experience. After exchanging a few words with a passing guardsman and returning to his patrol, he became aware of a strange shape coming towards him out of the darkness. To his amazement, he saw the outline of an enormous bear which appeared to materialise out of the tower door and rear up in front of him. Assuming he was being attacked by a real animal, the sentry drew his bayonet and struck out at the advancing apparition with such force that the great blade buried itself in the timber of the

Martin Tower door. As the phantom bear continued to advance, the soldier was overcome with fright and collapsed in a stupor, in which he was quickly discovered by a fellow guardsman who had heard something of the commotion. Most accounts suggest that the shock suffered by the hapless sentry was such that he never recovered and died only hours later. Wild animals were in fact kept in a menagerie at the Tower of London as late as 1834 and records exist of at least two bears living at widely different times: in 1251, a polar bear was given as a gift to Henry III by the King of Norway, while George II received a similar present, in this instance of a grizzly bear, from the Hudson Bay Company in 1811. This particular bear, known as 'Old Martin', eventually died at the new Regent's Park zoo in 1838, making it an unlikely candidate for the ghost bear of the Tower.

From the largest of British phantom animals to the smallest and most beautiful, a curious occurrence with a hint of the supernatural about it concerns the Georgian Theatre Royal in Bath, Somerset. During the theatre's 1948 pantomime season, Reg Maddox, the producer of *Little Red Riding Hood*, collapsed and died of a heart attack during an onstage rehearsal of a 'butterfly ballet' involving suitably painted scenery and a troupe of dancing girls dressed in butterfly costumes. Earlier in the day, a dead butterfly had been found on the stage and this, coupled with Maddox's tragic death, prompted the removal of the scene from the production. However, a few days before the show was due to open, a live tortoiseshell butterfly was seen fluttering around in the wings and the decision was made to restore the ballet scene on the opening night. Since then, the appearance of a butterfly inside the Theatre Royal is considered to be a portent of good luck to whatever production is being staged at the time, with the result that the *Little Red Riding Hood* butterfly scenery is kept hanging permanently in the fly tower. In 1979, a butterfly landed on the shoulder of television personality Leslie Crowther during a performance of *Aladdin*, and another was seen during a press call with actress Honor Blackman in 1985. As well as the Phantom Butterfly, the Theatre Royal boasts several other ghosts including a Grey Lady, often seen in the Dress Circle corridor accompanied by the distinctive scent of jasmine, an eighteenth-century doorman who only appears to members of the theatre cast, and a frightening apparition of a screaming man with multiple faces.

10

HAUNTED
OBJECTS

The idea that seemingly innocent items can be haunted by strange and sinister forces is one that has been used to great effect in both books and films, a number of which have become classics of their kind. The titular talisman from London-born author William Jacob's 1902 short story 'The Monkey's Paw' brings a mutilated factory worker back from the grave; 'The Skull of the Marquis de Sade', a short story written in 1965 by *Psycho* author Robert Bloch, was later made into a British horror film starring Peter Cushing and Christopher Lee, and a haunted piano eventually pushes a tormented concert pianist out of a window to his death in the 1967 Amicus multi-episode film, *Torture Garden*. Finally, the highly regarded *Dead of Night*, made by Ealing Studios in 1945, featured two sinister haunted objects: a possessed ventriloquist's dummy and an unearthly mirror, which shows the reflection of a strange room haunted by an evil and potentially murderous presence. Although not as deadly, the following real-life items all have ghostly stories to tell.

In the spring of 1959, a schoolboy from Fallowfield in Manchester claimed that his violin was haunted by the ghost of an old man named Nicholas. According to the young man's account, which was supported by his mother, a widower who also asserted she had heard ghostly music in the house on several occasions, an apparition would enter his bedroom during the night and play a rendition of Ravel's 'Bolero' before disappearing.

The haunting came to the attention of David Cohen, the Investigation Officer for the Manchester Psychical Research Society, a semi-spiritualist organisation. He visited the house and, after interviewing the family, obtained permission to hold regular séances on the premises in order to make contact with the ghostly Nicholas. The sittings took place for a period of two years, during which time Cohen claimed that a pair of ghostly hands complete with frilly lace cuffs regularly materialised and interacted with those present. In 1961, Cohen persuaded Sergeant Rowland Mason from the Greater Manchester Police's Fingerprint Bureau to attend a séance and obtain physical proof of Nicholas' existence by taking his fingerprints. Despite several attempts (which also included an attempt to photograph the ghost using an infra-red camera) the results were inconclusive and the case itself remains a mystery.

In December 1965, stories of a haunted walking stick dancing and rapping out popular tunes brought a paranormal circus of magicians and newspaper reporters to the bedside of a fourteen-year-old schoolboy from Barnsley, South Yorkshire. Not long after Michael Collindridge was confined to his bed in the Cranberry Hotel in Dodworth Road suffering from tonsillitis,

a Malacca-cane stick, previously belonging to an aunt used in the house to open window catches, began jumping and moving about by itself in full daylight behind the boy's headboard. As well as rapping out answers to questions put to it by both Michael and members of his family, the stick began tapping out the rhythms of songs such as 'Rule Britannia', 'Auld Lang Syne' and 'Jingle Bells', and on one occasion, after being put outside the bedroom on to the landing, was discovered the following morning stuck fast to the door. A town councillor, a professional conjuror from Rhyl and a local amateur magician all visited the house and were baffled by the phenomena. Reports appeared in *The People* and the *Sheffield Morning Telegraph* and the haunted stick (which had been X-rayed in Barnsley Hospital for hidden magnets) was even brought to the attention of television magician, David Nixon. The young Michael, despite being interested in magic tricks himself, insisted that the phenomena was genuine and could not explain what was controlling his aunt's walking stick. A few days later, the stick stopped its dancing for good.

In 1702, Thomas Busby was hanged for the murder of his father-in-law Daniel Awety, who was found beaten to death in woodland near his isolated farmhouse at Kirby Wiske in North Yorkshire. Busby's body was coated with pitch and gibbeted on the coaching road to Thirsk. Before his execution, he is said to have placed a curse on his favourite wooden chair to the effect that his ghost would return and have his revenge on anyone foolhardy enough to sit in it now he was no longer able to himself. The chair, which is now known as 'Busby's Stoop' and for many years resided in an old coaching inn of the same name in Kirby Wiske before being bequeathed to the Thirsk Museum, is said to have claimed many victims, including a Victorian chimney sweep, several airmen from the Royal Canadian Air Force stationed nearby during the Second World War, a builder's labourer and a brewery delivery driver. Despite the likelihood of the story being a twentieth-century invention, the haunted chair today hangs from the museum ceiling to prevent the possibility of any further supernatural fatalities.

A 200-year-old chair, on display in the much-haunted Baleroy Mansion in Chestnut Hill, Philadelphia, said to have once belonged to Napoleon and now haunted by the ghost of a woman named Amelia, is – like 'Busby's Stoop' – regarded as being a cursed object. Like its English counterpart, the chair is said to have led to the deaths of a number of people, including a former curator.

An eerie modern ghost story from the north of England is the strange tale of the Hexham Heads. Around the end of May 1971, eleven-year-old Colin Robson and his younger brother Leslie uncovered two cricket ball-sized stone heads in the garden of their house in Rede Avenue, Hexham. Later, Desmond Craigie, a Northumberland lorry driver who had lived in the house several years before, claimed he had made the objects as simple toys for his daughter Nancy, but when the heads were taken first to Newcastle Museum, and then sent to Southampton University for examination, Celtic scholar Dr Anne Ross declared they were in fact ancient artefacts that dated back to the second century AD. During the time that the heads were present in the Robsons' house, a series of unusual incidents took place, all of which appeared to be centred around the strange objects: the heads seemed to turn around and move by themselves, broken glass showered on to the bed of one of the Robson daughters in the manner of a poltergeist attack, while towards the end of the year there were accounts of a strange flower seen growing in the garden on the spot where the heads had been found, accompanied on at least one occasion by a mysterious glowing light. Most alarming was the bizarre apparition – part-animal, part-human, with a face similar to that of a sheep – which was seen inside the house by one of the neighbours. Curiously, archaeologist Anne Ross also claimed to have encountered a similar apparition in her own house in Southampton during the time that the heads were there for study. A definite age of the Hexham Heads was never determined and their whereabouts today remains a mystery.

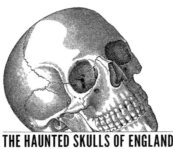

THE HAUNTED SKULLS OF ENGLAND

A number of buildings and locations around the country are associated with stories of screaming skulls and similar haunted death's heads. Most often, strange happenings such as unearthly noises, mysterious accidents and poltergeist-like activity are said to break out if these ancient and sinister relics are either touched or moved out of their respective resting places.

Two haunted skulls were for many years associated at first with the former Augustinian priory at Rushlake Green in East Sussex and later at the nearby Warbleton Priory Farm. In the early 1820s, an unnaturally preserved human head was said to have been discovered by a workman demolishing a section of brickwork in the priory ruins, and for many years was subsequently kept by a succession of tenants at the Priory Farm. Screams and other strange noises were said to plague the occupants of the house if the head (which by now had been reduced to a skull) was moved or taken out of the building and local cattle quickly fell ill. At some point the haunted skull was joined by a second death's head, said to be that of a man who murdered one of the tenant farmers. An alternative story credits both skulls as being those of two quarrelling monks who had fought and killed each other. For many years in the first half of the twentieth century, the skulls were apparently missing from Warbleton. Ghost hunter Robert Thurston Hopkins (1884–1958) claimed to have come across both on two separate occasions in an antique shop in Brighton before the Second World War, and today both are believed to be buried on the site of the old farm, possibly in a wall sealed in by two carved stone heads.

A haunted skull, said to be either that of a murdered serving girl or alternatively a young man killed by a drunken sea captain, is kept in the tap room at the seventeenth-century Ye Olde White Harte pub in Silver Street, Kingston upon Hull.

Inside a cupboard at Higher Farm in the village of Chilton Cantelo in Somerset resides the unquiet skull of Theophilus Broome, who died on 16 August 1670 at the age of sixty-nine. On his deathbed, Broome requested that his head be kept in the farmhouse he had known and loved in life while his body was consigned to a tomb in the nearby parish church of St James. In the 300 years following his death, there have seemingly been several attempts made to remove and bury the eerie relic, all of which are said to have been prevented by some form of supernatural intervention. These mysterious happenings include strange and disturbing noises inside the farmhouse itself as well as mishaps involving broken gravedigger's spades and similar omens of ill luck.

The early moated medieval manor house of Wardley Hall in Worsley, Greater Manchester, is home to another screaming skull: that of the English Benedictine monk and Catholic Saint, Ambrose Barlow, one of the Forty Martyrs of England and Wales, who was hung, drawn and quartered on 10 September 1641. Despite the historic provenance, tradition associates this particular skull with the Royalist rake, Roger Downes, who was said to have been beheaded in a fight in London and had his headless corpse thrown into the Thames. His severed head was then delivered in a wooden box to Wardley Hall, where it survived several attempts to remove it. On one occasion, a storm of such violence erupted after the skull was thrown into the moat that the hall's owners were obliged to drain the water and restore it to its usual resting place. As well as drowning, the skull is also said to have miraculously survived burning and burial.

'Owd Nance' was the name given to the skull of Anne Griffith, the daughter of Sir Henry Griffith, who in the early seventeenth century built Burton Agnes Hall, a manor house on the outskirts of Driffield in the East Riding of Yorkshire. Like Theophilus Broome at Chilton Cantelo, Anne requested that her head be removed to the house after her death, where it emitted blood-curdling screams every time an attempt was made to remove it from the premises. In 1900, 'Owd Nance' was permanently bricked up inside one of the walls of the house, after which her ghostly cries were heard no more.

The most famous of all England's screaming skulls is that associated with seventeenth-century Bettiscombe Manor near Sherborne in Dorset. In 1685, Squire Azariah Pinney was exiled to the West Indies after siding with James Scott during the West Country Rebellion. Many years later, Pinney's grandson, John Frederick Pinney, returned to his ancestral home accompanied by a black slave to whom he made a promise that on the servant's death, his body would be returned to Jamaica for burial with his family. Sadly the squire's edict went unfulfilled as John Frederick pre-deceased his servant and when the slave himself died a few weeks later, the promise was either forgotten or ignored and he was interred in St Stephen's churchyard, close to the grave of his former master. In the months that followed, strange noises and screams were heard coming from the servant's grave and the local crops and farm animals failed and fell ill. Eventually the skeleton was dug up and the skull removed to the manor house, after which the bizarre disturbances ceased. According to family tradition, the skull will cause the death within twelve months of anyone who takes it from the house, and similar agricultural problems to those reported during the period that the relic lay buried in the churchyard will befall the local farming community. When Frank Smyth interviewed Michael Pinney, a descendant at Bettiscombe in the early 1980s, he was told that a photographer at one point had carried the skull as far as the front door to get better lighting for a portrait but was prevented from going any further by the owner's wife, who quickly took the head back indoors.

Two haunted Derbyshire skulls are near neighbours of each other. At Tunstead Farm in the village of Tunstead Milton, on the road between Chapel-en-le-Frith and Whalley Bridge, resides 'Dickie', possibly the head of a murder victim that appears to be in the region of 400 years old. Like many of England's screaming skulls, Dickie has had his fair share of adventures. As well as being stolen and taken to the nearby village of Disley, the skull is also credited as having been thrown into the Coombes Reservoir and also buried on at least two occasions in the churchyard of the church of St Thomas Becket. The ensuing paranormal bedlam, both at Tunstead Farm and in the locale of its temporary resting places, ensured that Dickie was quickly returned. Approximately 15 miles south-east of Tunstead Milton, in the small village of Flagg, is the Flagg Hall skull, whose removal is likewise considered to bring about misfortune and local catastrophe.

☙ ☙ ☙

A strange story of a seemingly haunted relic exerting a mysterious force on the world of the living is the case of the 'Stolen Sacrum'. In 1936, Sir Alexander Hay Seton, informally known as 'Sandy', the 10th Baron of Abercorn and Armour Bearer to the Queen,

and his wife, Lady Zeyla Seton, undertook a sightseeing tour
of Egypt. The Setons were an ancient Scottish family and the
baronetcy originated during the reign of King James VI in the
mid-seventeenth century. Early one morning, the couple visited
a recently uncovered but nondescript tomb in the shadow of the
Great Pyramid, which was in the last stages of being cleared by
archaeologists. The tomb had belonged to a wealthy but nameless
Egyptian woman and inside the cramped and airless chamber
the Setons were able to view the occupant's skeleton, which was
laid out *in situ* on a stone slab. Back at their hotel that evening,
Zeyla Seton showed her husband what she described as a unique
souvenir which she had obtained inside the tomb earlier in the
day. Unobserved by either her husband or the Egyptian guide
who had accompanied them down into the burial chamber, Lady
Seton had removed a small triangular bone from the skeleton
as it lay in the shadows and this macabre relic, a pelvic sacrum
bone from the base of the spine, eventually accompanied the
couple back to their home, a modest three-storey terraced house
in Learmonth Gardens, Edinburgh. Unfortunately for the Setons,
their return to Scotland was the beginning of a series of strange
and frightening events, all of which seemed to be connected
with the presence of the stolen sacrum which Sir Alexander had
light-heartedly put on display in a glass-fronted case on a table
in the dining room. In the following months, the house became
plagued with strange noises, objects were moved and broken
and on several occasions a unidentified robed figure was seen
walking up the stairs into the upper part of the house. During
a dinner party, the sacrum appeared to jump by itself from a
table on to the floor and soon after, the room in which the bone
had been locked away was found ransacked by an unknown
intruder, despite Seton himself having the only key to the door.
Sir Alexander took the bone to the Edinburgh Psychic College
and told reporters that his wife was going to return it to the tomb
at Giza. 'I believe my family has been haunted by a sacred bone,'

Seton told a journalist from the *Daily Mirror*, 'this ghastly business has got to stop and we are taking no chances.' Despite the assurances, the trip was never made. The Setons' marriage foundered and eventually, after being exorcised by a priest from St Benedict's Abbey at Fort Augustus, the sacrum was burnt to ashes in the kitchen grate. Both Sir Alexander and Lady Zeyla Seton died in 1963: each felt that since the day they first set eyes on the mysterious sacrum, the haunted bone had exerted an evil influence over their lives.

11

PLANES, TRAINS AND OTHER HAUNTED TRANSPORT

The many paranormal reports and accounts that exist of soulless and material objects such as phantom coaches, spectral cars and ghostly ships lends weight to the stone tape theory (that ghosts are psychic recordings imprinted into the fabric of a place or location). This is certainly the case when the apparitions involved are those of the vehicles themselves. However, there are several reports of actual man-made vehicles that appear to have been haunted at one time or another by the ghostly presences of their former drivers, pilots and owners, supporting the idea that some essence of ourselves, be it a spirit or soul, lives on after physical death. This chapter includes several reports of both spectral and haunted vehicles.

PHANTOM PLANES AND GHOSTLY AVIATORS

The Northern Moors in the Peak District National Park in Derbyshire are haunted by phantom Second World War aircraft. In October 1982, a ghostly Lancaster Bomber was seen flying silently in full moonlight over the waters of the Ladybower

Reservoir by a married couple, David and Helen Shaw. In March 1997, at around 10 p.m., several witnesses saw a plane flying low over the moorland which appeared to crash into the ground and explode in a ball of orange flame. Despite an intensive ground and air search by emergency services which lasted for several hours, nothing was found and no aircraft had been reported missing across the region that day. The spectral Lancaster is thought to be the apparition of a bomber which crashed into the side of the 'Dark Peak' mountain on 18 May 1945 during a training flight, killing the crew of six airmen. A similar ghostly crash, witnessed by a local postman in 1995, is believed to be a USAF Dakota which came down in the same area in July 1945. The ghostly aeroplane made no sound as it passed overhead with its propellers turning before seemingly coming to earth in a farmer's field; again no wreckage of any description was found.

On several occasions during thunderstorms over the town of Weybridge in Surrey, people have reported hearing the sound of a biplane passing overhead. This is thought to be the ghost of an aviator, killed in a storm in the area in 1935.

In 1970, a tape recording made on the site of the old Bircham Newton aerodrome in Norfolk appeared to pick up the sound of a phantom aeroplane. The figure of a man in RAF uniform was seen on the viewing balcony of a squash court and poltergeist activity was also reported. The ghost is thought to be that of a Second World War airman named Wiley, who committed suicide on the base during an air raid. The old airbase, now a construction training college, was at one time also haunted by the sound of disembodied footsteps, a strange dragging sound and the apparition of a car containing a party of jovial airmen, which was seen to drive into the side of one of the aircraft hangers and disappear.

RAF Leeming in North Yorkshire is said to be the most haunted airfield in Britain. It was used as a bomber base during the Second World War and there were several crashes on and around the airfield, with many flying crews losing their lives. Apparitions of airmen wearing full flying kit were seen here on many occasions during the time it was used as an operational training base between 1950 and 1990. Ground crews and technical staff have also heard ghostly voices, as well as the sound of aircraft wheels taxiing across the runways at night when no scheduled flights were taking place.

A headless apparition dressed in a flying jacket haunts an industrial estate in Lichfield, Staffordshire. The ghost is believed to be a former airman killed in an accident with a rotor blade when the site was used as an RAF airfield and training station between 1940 and 1958.

The skies over the former RAF Aerodrome at Biggin Hill in Kent are haunted by the ghost of a lone Spitfire aircraft which has been seen and heard on warm summer evenings, its distinctive engine at full throttle, performing a victory roll on the approach to the airfield before fading away. The sound of the ghost plane is most often reported on 19 January. On the ground, ghostly figures in flying dress have been seen walking along the line of the old concrete Runway No. 21 and the sound of raised voices singing wartime songs have also been heard close by.

The aircraft museum at RAF Cosford in Shropshire is home to a famous haunted aeroplane. This is an Avro Lincoln bomber, serial number RF398, which was built in 1945 but never saw active service. The haunting dates from the late 1970s, when two staff members claimed to see an unidentified figure which disappeared suddenly near the aircraft. Since then, strange lights and the apparition of a young man in flying clothing has been seen inside the plane. Noises including footsteps and the sound of voices have also been recorded by ghost hunters carrying out controlled vigils on the bomber during the night.

In the early hours of 5 October 1930, the British airship R101, on its maiden flight to India, crashed into a hillside near the town of Beauvais in northern France, killing forty-six people. Three days later, at the London headquarters of ghost hunter Harry Price's National Laboratory of Psychical Research, medium Eileen Garrett, holding a séance in an attempt to contact the spirit of Sir Arthur Conan Doyle who had died on 7 July, began relaying messages which appeared to come from one of the dead R101 aircrew, Flight Lieutenant H. Carmichael Irwin. 'Irwin' passed on specific information concerning the recent crash, including technical specifications about the airship and the cause of the accident, which at the time were unknown to the general public. A transcript of the séance was sent by Price to Sir John Simon, who was heading an official enquiry into the disaster. It proved to be astonishingly accurate, containing information that was not known at the time, even to officials investigating at the crash site in France. Eileen Garrett had had several premonitions that the R101 would crash and Major Oliver Villiers, a close friend of Sir Sefton Brancker, the British Director of Civil Aviation, was convinced that the crash information had come from the dead Lieutenant Irwin.

On 29 December 1972, American Eastern Air Lines Flight 401, a Lockheed L-1011-1 TriStar jet, crashed into marshland in the Florida Everglades shortly after beginning its approach into Miami International Airport, killing 163 people, including Captain Robert Loft, First Officer Albert Stockstill and Flight Engineer Donald Repo. An air accident investigation concluded that the flight crew had become distracted by an inoperative landing gear indicator light and were unaware that the autopilot mechanism had become disengaged, causing the aircraft to gradually lose altitude. During the following year, rumours began circulating around the airline company that the ghosts of members of the Flight 401 cabin crew, in particular Robert Loft and Donald Repo, had been seen by staff on other company aircraft, most noticeably planes that had been fitted with serviceable parts salvaged from the wreckage of the doomed TriStar. The figure of Captain Loft, wearing his full flight uniform, was seen sitting in the first-class section during the course of one flight, while the apparition of Donald Repo was allegedly seen several times, once in a galley reflected in an oven door, and on another occasion sitting at the flight deck; Repo is said to have spoken to members of Eastern Air Lines staff, warning them about potential safety issues and his voice was heard over the public address system during flight. The case was publicised by researcher John G. Fuller whose best-selling book, *The Ghost of Flight 401*, was published in 1976. Eastern Air Lines was dissolved in 1991 and constantly denied that a haunting ever took place. Despite this, the case remains popular and well known.

On 3 March 1948, a Sabena Douglas DC3 crashed in fog on the runway at Heathrow Airport in West London, killing twenty-five people. For several years afterwards, there were reports that a phantom figure wearing a bowler hat had been seen walking on and near the site of the accident on the No. 1 runway. He is thought to be one of the crash victims, who first appeared to rescue workers immediately after the accident asking for his lost briefcase. A body matching that of the apparition was said to have been recovered from the wreckage a short time afterwards.

One morning in June 1995, airline captain Robert Hambleton-Jones, a former fighter pilot, was walking through the concourse at Glasgow Airport when he saw a friend and fellow pilot, Robert Macleod, walking towards him. 'How's it going, you old bastard?' Macleod said cheerily and the two men stood chatting for several minutes. Eventually, Macleod said 'I must go', and the airmen parted. As Captain Hambleton-Jones picked up his bags and looked round, he saw that his friend was now nowhere in sight. The following day, a colleague showed Hambleton-Jones a newspaper in which was a stunning piece of information: Robert Macleod's obituary. The pilot had died at his home in Edinburgh of a sudden heart attack at the age of thirty-eight four days before. At the time the two men had met on the concourse,

Macleod's body was in fact in the airport being transported back to his home town. The case was investigated by Scottish researcher Archie Roy (*see* Chapter 13) who was convinced the airline captain had encountered the post-mortem apparition of his dead friend.

GHOST TRAINS AND HAUNTED RAILWAYS

On the evening of 28 December 1879, a violent storm tore down a section of the Tay Bridge across the Firth of Tay south of Dundee in Scotland: seventy-five passengers and crew on a night train from Edinburgh crossing the bridge at the moment the structure was wrecked were killed when the locomotive and carriages plunged into the icy water below. Over the years, a gleaming phantom train is reported to have been seen on the anniversary of the disaster, crossing the new Tay Bridge, which was opened on 13 July 1887.

Another Scottish ghost train haunts the old railway station at Dunphail in the Highlands. On New Year's Eve 1921, two local men claimed to have seen a locomotive and carriages with all lights on but with no one on board thunder through the station after the last train had left for the night. Since then the phantom steam train has made other appearances, one of the latest occurrences taking place in 2009 when two American tourists saw what they assumed at first was a real train pass silently through the disused station before fading away.

One of the most famous ghost trains is the spectral recreation of the funeral cortège of assassinated American president, Abraham Lincoln, which transported his body across seven states between Washington, D.C. and Springfield, Illinois, on 21 April to 3 May 1865. Along the way, the president's body was viewed by thousands of citizens in Baltimore, Maryland; Harrisburg and Philadelphia, Pennsylvania; New York City; Albany and Buffalo, New York State; Cleveland and Columbus, Ohio; Indianapolis and Michigan City, Indiana; and Chicago and Springfield in Illinois. Lincoln is said to have had a premonition of his own death, describing a vivid dream a fortnight before he was shot down by John Wilkes Booth, in which he came across a coffin laid out on a funeral bier inside the White House. Tradition has it that on the anniversary of the assassination, a phantom steam train complete with an orchestra of skeletons follows the same route, stopping all the station clocks as it passes on its way. When not riding in his death train, Lincoln's ghost is reported to haunt the White House itself, where a number of people including Queen Wilhelmina of the Netherlands, Maureen Reagan (daughter of Ronald Reagan), President Harry S. Truman and seamstress Lillian Rogers Parks all claimed to have seen and heard strange things including footsteps, knocks and raps, as well as the presence and apparition of Lincoln himself.

Bincombe Tunnel, on the Weymouth to Dorchester line in Dorset, is haunted by the figure of a man walking with bowed head, seen by several train drivers in the early 1990s. The ghost may possibly be that of a young signal box man, Sidney Watts, who was struck down while walking home through the tunnel on 8 August 1883, aged twenty-four.

A ghostly white cat is said to haunt Yarwell Tunnel on the Nene Valley Railway at Wansford in Cambridgeshire. According to tradition, the animal, known as Snowy, once belonged to the Yarwell stationmaster who was knocked down and killed one night while out searching for his missing pet. Snowy's ghost, rather than that of his unfortunate owner, returns to the scene of the accident from time to time.

GHOSTS OF THE LONDON UNDERGROUND

Opened in January 1863, the London Underground is now regarded as one of the most haunted railway networks in Britain. There are many allegedly haunted stations and incidents of both railway staff and passengers experiencing ghostly phenomena. An apparition of a Victorian male, dressed in traditional stovepipe hat, frock coat and wearing gloves, seen on many occasions walking in the vicinity of Covent Garden station, is traditionally assumed to be the ghost of actor William Terriss, who was stabbed to death in the lobby of the Adelphi Theatre by Richard Archer Prince, also an actor, on 16 December 1897. Another apparition, that of an elderly woman dressed in black – the so-called Black Nun – who haunts Bank tube station, is thought to be that of the deluded Sarah Whitehead who, unable to accept that her brother, an employee at the Bank of England, had been executed for forgery in the early nineteenth century, called at the bank every day for nearly forty years asking for him by name. Sarah's ghost has also been seen walking along a pathway in the garden behind the Bank of England building, where she was buried when it was originally the graveyard attached to the old parish church of St Christopher-le-Stocks. This was demolished to make way for an extension to the bank in 1781. Ghostly figures have also been seen at the Elephant & Castle, where the footsteps of an invisible runner sound along the line; the disused British Museum station, where the apparition of an Ancient Egyptian complete with headdress and loincloth made newspaper headlines in the 1930s; Liverpool Street, where the figure of a man wearing white overalls was seen by staff on CCTV after the station was closed for the night; and King's Cross St Pancras, haunted by a screaming woman in modern-day clothing. Passengers on the Bakerloo line have reported seeing a figure sitting beside them reflected in the window glass, despite the seat next to them being empty, while the sounds of screaming women and children have also been reported from Bethnal Green tube station, where 173 people were crushed and suffocated to death during an air-raid test on 3 March 1943.

💀 💀 💀

An interesting variation on the haunted railway theme is the ghostly black smoke which was seen billowing out of the Ingro Tunnel at Keighley in West Yorkshire.

In 1936, the disused Cliddesden station on the old Basingstoke and Alton Light Railway in Hampshire was used for location filming for the Will Hay comedy, *Oh! Mr Porter*, itself based on *Dad's Army* actor Arnold Ridley's famous 1923 play, *The Ghost Train*. Something of the film's supernatural subplot appears to survive, as in recent years the sound of a steam locomotive passing through the deserted station has been heard on several occasions.

One of the most persistent railway ghosts is the White Lady who haunts the site of Platform No. 2 at the former Maldon East station in Essex. In the late 1950s, the stationmaster's wife claimed to have seen the figure on a number of occasions, noting that it groaned eerily as it walked, accompanied by an intensely cold atmosphere. The Beeching axe closed the Witham and Woodham Ferrers lines and as a result Maldon East in 1964, after which the White Lady continued to be seen in the impressive Victorian station building which was converted into a restaurant.

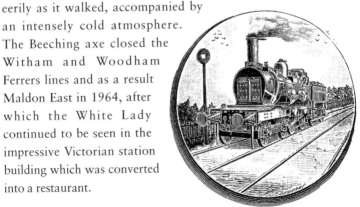

GHOSTLY CARS AND OTHER MOTORISED TRANSPORT

In March 1961, Stanley Prescott of Kingsbury Gardens, Dunstable, in Bedfordshire, was driving near the 'Travellers Rest' crossroads near Edlesborough in neighbouring Buckinghamshire when a black Morris saloon appeared to materialise out of nowhere and drove at speed straight at his car. Swerving to avoid a collision, Prescott lost control and crashed through a hedgerow into a field. Recovering, he realised that the stretch of road was now empty and that there was no sign of the phantom saloon. The driver's wife, a passenger in the same car, saw nothing.

The hill road from Sligachan on the Isle of Skye is haunted by the apparition of a 1934 Austin motor car which appears driving at high speed with headlights blazing but with no driver at the wheel. It was seen on several occasions after the Second World War, once by a local postman and on another occasion by GP Dr Allan MacDonald. All witnesses agree that the vehicle, which moves too quickly for a normal car, vanishes as suddenly as it appears and that the driver's seat is quite empty.

The apparition of a broken-down car has been known to cause a number of minor accidents on the A41 dual carriageway on the outskirts of Watford in Hertfordshire.

Two roads around Dartmoor in Devon are haunted by phantom cars. On the A379 near Modbury, a black 1920 Daimler Laudaulette was seen by a driver and disappeared as he approached it. Another ghostly car of unknown type has also been reported on the B3212 road near Moretonhampstead. Further along the same road, between Postbridge and Two Bridges, is a stretch of highway haunted by Devon's most famous road ghost, the prehistoric-sounding Hairy Hands of Dartmoor. Not encountered with any frequency today, there was a time in the late 1960s when drivers reported the unsettling experience of feeling an unseen presence in the vehicle with them and having the steering wheel wrenched from their grasp. On several extreme occasions, the physical disturbance was accompanied by the appearance of two disembodied hands, said to be covered with a matting of hair, which materialised and gripped the wheel.

Just outside the village of Brandon in Warwickshire on the A428, a phantom lorry has been seen careering off of the road at speed near a sharp bend in the highway.

The road at Clouds Hill near Wareham in Dorset is haunted by the sound of a phantom motorcycle. This is thought to be the ghost of T.E. Lawrence, 'Lawrence of Arabia', who was killed here on his Brough Superior machine on 19 May 1935, aged forty-six. Lawrence's nearby cottage is also said to be haunted by his apparition, which has been seen wearing shining desert robes.

One of the most famous British road ghost hauntings took place in the mid-1930s in the Ladbroke Grove area of West London. The apparition of an empty No. 7 Routemaster bus was seen driving late at night, long after the normal bus service had finished, particularly near the junction of St Mark's Road and Cambridge Gardens, where a blind corner was widely held to be an accident black spot. A London Transport official claimed he saw the phantom bus – with all interior and headlights on but devoid of crew or passengers – pull up silently into the bus depot and then vanish. Ghost hunter Frank Smyth, who collected reports of the haunting in the 1970s, noted that once the local council had made improvements to the road junction by repositioning an adjacent wall, the ghostly No. 7 bus, considered locally to be a portent of ill omen, was never seen again.

PHANTOM HITCHHIKERS AND GHOSTLY PEDESTRIANS

Not all road hauntings involve supernatural cars, buses and other spectral vehicles. There are many reports of encounters with phantom pedestrians and similar paranormal road users.

The stretch of the A5 trunk road close to The Pack Horse Inn south of Markyate in Bedfordshire is haunted by the figure of a solitary cricketer. One Sunday morning in 1970, a taxi driver was forced to break violently when a tall white figure stepped out from the hedgerow immediately in front of his car. Convinced he had knocked the man down, he pulled to a halt but there was no sign of any casualty and the taxi was undamaged. The ghost is believed to be one of two men killed in a fatal accident in 1958 on the same stretch of road, when a coach carrying a Surrey works cricket team returning from a match in Milton Bryan collided with an overtaking car.

One of Britain's most well-known modern ghost stories took place near the village of Stanbridge in Bedfordshire in the late 1970s. Late in the evening of 12 October 1979, twenty-six-year-old carpet fitter Roy Fulton was returning home from a darts match in Leighton Buzzard when he stopped to give a lift to a young man standing on an isolated stretch of Station Road on the outskirts of Dunstable. The youth got into Fulton's Mini van and remained silent as they drove off. After a few minutes, Fulton turned to offer his passenger a cigarette and was stunned to find that he had completely vanished. Terrified, the workman drove 'like a bat out of hell' to his local pub, the Glider in Lowther Road, Dunstable, where he told the entire incredible story. Later Fulton visited the local police station and reported the incident. The police confirmed no accident had taken place on or near the spot in recent years and the incident remains unexplained.

In 1965, musicians Peter Green and Mick Fleetwood, who would later go on to form the internationally successful rock group Fleetwood Mac, were returning to London from a club gig in Portsmouth. As they passed through the village of Cobham in the early hours of the morning, the two men, along with their driver and fellow band members Peter Bardens and David Ambrose, all became aware of a bizarre figure gliding in the roadway ahead. They later described seeing an almost impossibly tall person, well over 7ft tall, dressed in a long mackintosh. The face was that of an elderly man, but somehow the eyes appeared to be missing and the entire apparition seemed to radiate its own illumination. The van passed near to the figure, which appeared to be oblivious to the vehicle's presence. Shaken by the incident, none of the men felt inclined to investigate further and continued on their way. Whether this eerie ghost man has been seen again in the same area is unclear.

The ghost of a young woman, said to be the victim of a motorcycle accident, has been seen by drivers passing along the B2150 Hulbert Road on the outskirts of Havant in Hampshire.

One evening in the summer of 1987, Graham Brooke, a builder who at the time was training for a marathon, accompanied by his son Nigel, was running along the old Pennine road at Stocksbridge in South Yorkshire. At the time, the construction of the A616 bypass between Manchester and Sheffield around the town was underway and, unbeknown to the two men, reports of a strange monk-like figure seen in the vicinity of the new Pearoyd Lane bridge had been circulating in the area. Two security guards employed by the McAlpine construction company and two policemen, Dick Ellis and John Beet, all claimed to have had strange experiences there at night. As the two runners made their way along the road they both saw a man dressed in old-fashioned-looking clothes and trailing a large bag coming towards them. Unnervingly, the figure's face appeared black and featureless and as they drew closer they saw that the man appeared to be walking in the road itself as he was only visible from the knees up. As Brooke turned to speak to his son, both became aware that the man had vanished, leaving behind an unpleasant musty smell.

Ghostly incidents connected with the eerie case of the Blue Bell Hill Girl date back to the mid-1970s. In July 1974, Maurice Goodenough, a thirty-five-year-old bricklayer, claimed to have knocked down a mysterious female pedestrian while driving at night on a section of the old A229 road at Blue Bell Hill between Maidstone and Chatham in Kent. The unknown woman, who appeared suddenly in front of his car, disappeared after the shocked motorist went to fetch help. In 1992, the Blue Bell Hill Girl was seen again. Just before midnight on Sunday 8 November, coach driver Ian Sharpe, who was driving his car along the new dual carriageway around Blue Bell Hill, saw the figure of a woman standing in the middle of the road. She refused to move out of the way as he approached at speed and appeared to vanish beneath the bonnet of his vehicle. Sharpe was unable to find a casualty by the roadside and in a distraught state reported the incident to the local police. Two weeks later, nineteen-year-old Chris Dawkins was returning home from a day at Brands Hatch along the Old Chatham Road around 1½ miles north of the spot where Ian Sharpe had his encounter when a young woman suddenly appeared from between two parked cars and ran straight into the path of his car. Dawkins later described the woman turning and smiling at him as she dropped down and disappeared from sight. When the young man got out of his car, he found the figure had completely vanished. Tradition has it that the ghost is that of a young woman killed in a car accident on the eve of her wedding on the old A229 road in 1965. The earliest report of a phantom hitchhiker at Blue Bell Hill dates back to 1966, when a local man claimed to have picked up a woman who asked to be taken to an address in Maidstone, which later turned out to be that of the tragic young bride-to-be.

A phantom hitchhiker story from London occurred in October 1972. A motorcyclist offered a lift to a young man standing beside the Greenwich entrance to the original Victorian

Blackwall Tunnel who had vanished from the pillion by the time they had crossed under the Thames to the northern Tower Hamlets side. Frightened that his passenger has fallen from the machine, the rider went back through the tunnel a total of four times but the person was gone. As with the case of the Blue Bell Hill Girl in Kent, when the motorcyclist went to the address given to him by the ghostly youth, he apparently learnt that a man matching his description had once lived there but had been dead for several years.

☙ ☙ ☙

One Sunday morning in 1987, eighteen-year-old Donna Barnett was driving along Abbey Barn Lane, a single-track road near High Wycombe in Buckinghamshire, when she noticed a small blue Fiat car coming towards her. A dark-haired man was at the wheel, with a female passenger. Having come to a halt, Donna reversed back a short distance into a passing place and, on looking ahead, was amazed to see that the Fiat together with its occupants had completely vanished: the car had not passed her and there was nowhere the other driver could have turned off or reversed out of sight in time. The origins of this phantom car remain a mystery.

During the Second World War, Knebworth House in Hertfordshire was used as a transit station for British tanks. The road outside the lodge gates leading to nearby Codicote is now haunted by the apparition of a Churchill tank, which appears with the turret hatch open and the figure of a steel-helmeted soldier gesturing for those on the roadway to take cover, presumably from a German air raid. At Bovington Camp Tank Museum, near Wareham in Dorset, a German Tiger tank is haunted by the ghost of a former occupant: the apparition of a man has been seen in and around the museum building, often looking through the windows at the wartime vehicle.

PHANTOM COACHES AND OTHER HORSE-DRAWN VEHICLES

Many phantom coaches are traditionally associated with portents of death and disaster. A large black funeral hearse with a headless coachman and pulled by headless black horses is said to travel the B651 road near the hamlet of St Paul's Walden to the west of Stevenage. Its appearance was considered to be an omen of impending death to someone living nearby.

Hatfield House on the northern outskirts of London, a Jacobean mansion built in 1611 by Robert Cecil, the 1st Earl of Salisbury, is haunted by perhaps the most reckless of all of England's phantom coaches. The ghostly carriage materialises outside the main gates and travels at speed towards the building, where it passes through the main doors and continues up the main staircase before fading away. Interestingly enough, Wolfeton House, a medieval and Elizabethan mansion near Yeovil in Dorset, has an almost identical haunting: in this instance, the spectral coach, which also passes up the grand staircase before melting into the panelling, is driven by Thomas Trenchard, who built Wolfeton with his father, John Trenchard, in the late fifteenth century.

One night in 1985, Paul Green and a fellow angler were fishing for carp on Startops Reservoir, one of the large man-made lakes feeding the Grand Union Canal on the outskirts of Tring in Hertfordshire. Tring has been described (by local historian Sheila Richards) as the most haunted town in Hertfordshire, and the experiences of Green and his friend certainly help to support this. After setting up a makeshift bivouac on the shore of the reservoir, both men had settled down under their umbrellas and had been fishing for some time when they heard the sound of something approaching them from out of the darkness. Both were astonished to see what appeared to be a black coach pulled by horses moving along the top of a retaining wall next to the water's edge. As they watched, the vehicle pulled to a halt, the side door nearest to them opened and a man wearing a tricorn hat stepped out and appeared to walk down into the water, where he disappeared from sight. After this, the vision of the coach with its horses and driver melted away, as did the two anglers: both men, shaken by their experience, packed up their equipment and fled.

The night of 31 May is a busy one where phantom coach hauntings are concerned. A mustard-coloured coach driven by the Duke de Morrow is said to career down the driveway of Hill Hall near Theydon Bois in Essex, an Elizabethan mansion subsequently used in the second half of the twentieth century as a women's prison before being refurbished as apartments.

At Potter Heigham in Norfolk, at the stroke of midnight, a ghostly coach with sparks flying from its wheels is said to cross the old bridge over the River Thurne before crashing and disappearing into the water, while on the same night in County Antrim, a black coach is associated with the ruins of Massereene Castle on the shores of Lough Neagh in Northern Ireland.

On Christmas Eve, a ghostly coach-and-four with a headless groom on the box, rides to the entrance of the sixteenth-century Roos Hall on the outskirts of Beccles in Suffolk, considered by some to be the most haunted house in East Anglia. A few days later, on New Year's Eve, when the water of the Loch of Skene in Aberdeenshire is frozen, a phantom carriage is said to appear and cross from one side to the other.

PHANTOM SHIPS AND OTHER SEAFARING HAUNTINGS

Early in December 1924, James Courtney and Michael Meehan, two crewmen from the oil tanker SS *Watertown* were apparently suffocated by poisonous fumes while cleaning out a cargo tank on board the ship. Soon after they were buried at sea and as the tanker made its way through the Panama Canal, several members of the crew, including the captain, reported seeing the ghostly faces of the two men following behind in the ship's wake. When the Watertown docked in New Orleans, the happenings were reported to the ship's owners, the Cities Service Company, and it was decided that, if the eerie heads returned, an attempt should be made to photograph the ghosts. On the next voyage, the heads of the two dead men were again seen to be following behind the tanker and Captain Tracy took six photographs which were later developed on their return. Five of the pictures showed only waves; however, in the sixth photograph, now one of the most famous ghost photographs, two clear heads can be seen floating on the water. In 2010, researcher Blake Smith, who spent several months examining the case, came to the conclusion that the picture had in fact been faked and that the story of the two dead seamen was a hoax. The most likely explanation, according to Smith, was that one of the heads was a genuine simulacrum and that the second head had been added into the picture and the ghost story created around it.

Breydon Water at Great Yarmouth in Norfolk is said to be haunted by an hour-long procession of ghostly galleons which materialise just after midnight on 11 July each year.

Porthcurno Cove near St Leven in Cornwall is haunted by the *Goblin*, a black, square-rigged ghost ship that glides through the water heading for the beach. When it reaches the shore, the vessel is said to continue on its way across dry land for some distance before eventually fading away.

Off the coast of St Ives, another Cornish ghost ship, believed to be the schooner *Neptune*, wrecked in a storm on 17 April 1838, has been seen. Before the *Neptune* was lost, another unknown ghost ship was said to have appeared in the bay as a portent of the forthcoming disaster.

The waters around Block Island, situated 10 miles off the coast of Rhode Island, are haunted by America's most famous ghost ship, the *Palatine*, which according to local legend ran aground en route to Philadelphia during a storm in 1752, while carrying a living cargo of Dutch settlers eager to make a fresh start for themselves in the New World. The wreck was looted by the island fisherman and then set alight, trapping a female passenger on board who was burnt to death. On many occasions since then, a strange light, said to be the ghostly *Palatine*, has been sighted around Christmas time: in 1882 the *Scientific American* carried a lengthy report given by the owner of a Long Island fishing boat, and there were several sightings during the winter of 1969. Despite being immortalised in a poem by Quaker poet John Greenleaf Whittier, the story of the *Palatine* is in fact a fabrication and based on the real shipwreck of the *Princess Augusta*, which took place in 1738. The mysterious *Palatine* Light, however, continues to be regarded as one of America's great 'spook light' hauntings.

The legend of the *Flying Dutchman*, the most famous ghost ship of all, dates back over 200 years to the late eighteenth century. Regarded as an omen of disaster, the *Dutchman*, which can never make port and is doomed to sail the oceans of the world forever, will try to signal messages from its crew to people long dead whenever it is encountered. Among many purported sightings is one by George, Prince of Wales, later King George V, and his elder brother, Prince Albert Victor, Duke of Clarence, off the coast of Australia between Melbourne and Sydney in 1881. Around thirteen people from three separate ships all reported seeing the phantom vessel and a few hours later, the *Dutchman*'s curse ran true when a yardman fell from the foretopmast crosstrees and was killed. Karl Dönitz, Commander-in-Chief of the German Navy, also reported seeing the ghost ship while on a tour of duty east of Suez.

The SS *Great Eastern*, an iron sailing steam passenger ship designed by the famous engineer Isambard Kingdom Brunel in the mid-1850s, was an unlucky vessel whose troubled career is often put down to a ghostly curse. Problems plagued the *Great Eastern* from the very start. After several failed attempts, she was launched in London on 31 January 1858 and was, at the time, the largest ship ever built. However, on her maiden voyage from London to Weymouth, a huge explosion destroyed one of the funnels and several stokers working below decks were killed. The vessel's owners, the Great Ship Company, suffered constant financial problems and during a voyage to America in September 1861, the ship was badly damaged in a storm and lost its port paddle wheel. Two years later she ran aground and was again damaged while approaching New York harbour. The *Great Eastern* spent her final years as a cable-laying ship before being broken up and scrapped in the late 1880s. As the vast double iron hull was being taken apart, two human skeletons dressed in rags, those of a man and a boy, were allegedly found trapped inside the cavity. They were said to be the bodies of a riveter and a child worker, who went missing during the time that the ship was being built many years before. According to tradition, many of the ship's crew reported hearing strange hammering noises while the ship was at sea, which woke sailors in their bunks and was loud enough to be felt even during stormy weather.

12

GHOSTS ACROSS THE WORLD

The British Isles have been evocatively described by the novelist and historian Peter Ackroyd as 'a land engulfed by mist and twilight', and it is true that this country is regarded by the international paranormal community as one of the most haunted in the world. However, there are many well-known and impressive ghost stories and supernatural experiences which have been recorded over the years from all over the world, while the advent of the Internet in recent years has resulted in Western ghost hunters becoming aware of many interesting and convincing haunted locations in other countries including India, Russia and the Far East. Here is a selection of unusual and unnerving supernatural encounters from both home and abroad.

In 1959, Revd R.S. Blance visited Corroboree Rock, a remote site 20 miles east of Alice Springs in Australia's Northern Territory, where native aborigines once held sacrificial rituals. Blance claimed he was alone at the time and took a number of colour photographs. When developed, one of his pictures contained a remarkable 'extra', a clear semi-materialised figure wearing long robes and with a domed head and skull-like face. The photograph appears not to have been manipulated in any way and the Corroboree Spirit remains unexplained.

In the late 1980s, the former colliery at Cotgrave in Nottinghamshire was said to be haunted by the ghost of a groaning man. A nineteen-year-old miner, Gary Pine, claimed he

had encountered a figure wearing dark overalls and a black helmet while working alone in one of the underground galleries, which had walked through a pile of sacks and then vanished into a dead-end passageway. Pine was so upset by this experience that he was given sick leave and for several weeks other miners on shifts near the haunted tunnel would only work there in pairs.

An unexplained case of poltergeist stone throwing took place in the Brooklyn suburb of Wellington, New Zealand in 1963. At around 9.30 p.m. on 24 March, numerous small stones and pennies began to rain down on the Ohiro Lodge guest house: twelve windows were broken and one boarder and a policeman were struck during the bombardment, which lasted for most of the night. Despite the area being searched by over thirty people, no normal explanation came to light. The next night, the Ohiro Lodge Poltergeist struck again. On this occasion, stones began hitting the sides of the building around two hours before the previous assault had begun and lasted until well after midnight. On the third and final night, over 200 local residents joined a squad of police officers staking out the guest house, who deployed radar equipment and tracker dogs in the hope of catching what they believed to be a group of thrill seekers armed with catapults. A two-and-a-half hour attack petered out around 9.00 p.m. and, despite much activity, the authorities were again none the wiser. The guest house owner, Mr Beatty, later claimed that the problem began after he had cut down sections of some trees which were growing in front of the building and that after an elderly Maori woman had exorcised an evil spirit which had been angered by the tree felling, the poltergeist departed and peace returned to the little hotel.

THE FACES IN THE FLOOR

On 23 August 1971, a strange mark appeared on the concrete floor in the kitchen of a farmhouse in the village of Bélmez de la Moraleda in Andalucia, Spain. Over the course of a week the mark changed into the image of a ghostly human face that frightened the owner's wife, Mrs Maria Pereira, to the point that she ordered her son to destroy it. The floor was broken up and relaid, but soon another face appeared in the new cement. When this was cut out by workmen from the local council and taken away for examination, a third face quickly replaced it, which established a pattern: as soon as one face was removed, more appeared to take its place. The Pereira home, dubbed 'The House of the Faces', soon became famous and people began to flock to the village to experience the phenomenon for themselves. The eerie Bélmez Faces continued to regularly appear for several years – one face, which appeared in June 1972, lasted many months and appeared to regularly change its expression. Many local villagers considered them to be supernatural in origin, particularly as excavation work under part of the kitchen floor discovered human bones, possibly part of an ancient cemetery; a small church stood quite close to the house. A researcher, José Romero, believed they were in fact 'thoughtographic' projections, images created by the psychic mind of Mrs Pereira when in a state of anxiety or similarly disturbed mental condition. However, a sceptical report, published in 1993, suggested that the faces were in fact painted forgeries and after Mrs Pereira's death in 2004, two Spanish journalists accused her son Diego of faking the ghosts in order to bring visitors into the town. As such, the Bélmez Faces remain controversial to this day.

☙ ☙ ☙

Pawleys Island on America's South Carolina coast is traditionally haunted by the apparition of a faceless grey man whose appearance is said to be an indication of an approaching storm. The ghost, possibly that of Percival Pawley who was the first to settle on the island and after whom it was named, is said to have appeared in 1822, 1883, 1916, 1954 and 1955, and on each occasion a violent hurricane hit the area a few hours later.

In 1979, police motorcyclist Mahmood Ali gave a lift to an attractive young woman wearing a white dress in the Peshawar district of Pakistan. The girl gave an address to where she wanted to be taken but, not long after setting off, Ali realised that he was suddenly alone on the back of the machine: his companion had simply vanished. Making investigations, the policeman discovered that a fatal motor accident had taken place at the spot where he had picked up the hitchhiker and that a photograph of the victim, a twenty-year-old girl, in the police files matched the ghostly girl exactly.

Before the 2003 film *Pirates of the Caribbean* made ghost ships and buccaneering phantoms fashionable, one the Caribbean's best-known hauntings was that of Rose Hall Plantation near Montego Bay on the island of Jamaica. The house itself, a Georgian mansion built in the 1770s was, according to popular accounts, the home of plantation owner John Palmer and his wife, Rosa for over forty years. At the beginning of May 1790, Rosa Palmer died suddenly and sometime later, John Palmer, now in his early seventies, married twenty-eight year old 'white witch' Annie, who ruled Rose Hall with a sadistic hand, torturing and tormenting the slaves. After John Palmer's death, Annie was shunned by her former husband's associates and was eventually murdered in her bed during a revolt by the plantation workers. For many years her ghost was said to haunt the house and its grounds, pushing the unwary to their deaths down the deserted staircases, accompanied by eerie screams and muffled cries of terror. Rose Hall itself was restored during the 1960s and is today a popular tourist destination.

Another well-known Caribbean haunting concerns the parish church at Christ Church, Barbados, and the haunted or 'creeping' coffins of the Chase family vault. In July 1812, when the vault was opened to lay Dorcas Chase to rest, the previously interred coffins – all cased in lead – of former family members Thomasina Goddard and Mary Anna Maria Chase (an infant) were found in disarray inside the underground chamber, having moved from their original positions. The coffins were repositioned and the vault sealed. A month later, on 9 August 1812, the head of the family, Thomas Chase, died and the vault was reopened. The mourners noted all within was as it had been left previously and after the new coffin was placed inside, the tomb was again sealed. Just over four years later, on 25 September 1816, when the coffin of a child, Samuel Brewster Ames, was placed inside the vault, the four resident caskets were found to have moved, as was the case on 17 November of the same year when the body of a relation (also called Samuel Brewster) was transferred from a cemetery in the nearby parish of St Philip. Now a well-known mystery across the island, a large crowd gathered on 17 July 1819 for what was to be the haunted vault's final burial, that of Thomasina Clarke. The several hundred spectators were not disappointed as again the previously interred caskets were found to have been disturbed and lay scattered around the interior of the tomb. In April of the following year, a commission

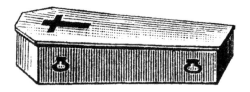

of officials led by Viscount Combermere decided to investigate the haunting and the Chase vault was reopened. The six coffins inside were again in confusion, having apparently turned by themselves nearly 180 degrees, so that they were facing in the opposite direction to that in which they had been previously left. Following the latest discovery, it was decided to abandon the vault and all of its occupants were removed and buried in another part of the churchyard. The Chase vault survives and today remains open and unused.

HAUNTINGS IN INDIA

A vast country, India has many interesting and atmospheric locations with haunted reputations, several of which are connected with the years of the British Raj. Like many foreign hauntings, they remain little known outside the country.

Lothian Cemetery, the oldest burial ground in Delhi, India's largest city, is said to be haunted by the headless ghost of a British soldier who committed suicide over an affair with a local Indian woman.

An abandoned workers' town at Mussoonie in the northern Indian state of Uttarakhand is considered to be one of India's most haunted places. Connected with the former Lambi Dehar strip mine which was closed in the early 1990s, the empty and decaying buildings are said to be haunted by a frightening witch-like apparition that wanders the hillsides at night. Passers-by have also claimed to hear voices coming from the ruins at night and the nearby roads are also considered to be accident black spots.

The Poona Poltergeist case took place in the late 1920s and involved two orphaned brothers, Damodar and Ramkrishna Bapat, who were adopted by a wealthy publisher, Dr Ketkar and his wife. Both boys were affected, first it was just Ramkrishna, but from April 1928 onwards, his younger brother – who was the most affected out of the two – was also involved. The disturbances lasted until October 1930, after which they stopped completely. The case involved the full range of poltergeist phenomena and was particularly well documented in the diaries of two contemporary witnesses, the family doctor and Dr Ketkar's sister-in-law. Objects were thrown and broken, windows smashed and items appeared and disappeared. The poltergeist also ate some fruit left out for it as a peace offering and on several occasions, Damodar Bapat claimed to have been levitated and transported into a car which stood inside a closed garage.

The Taj Mahal Hotel, also known as the Hotel Grand Palace, in Mumbai, brought to international attention by a terrorist outrage in 2008, is traditionally haunted by the ghost of its former architect whose apparition has been seen by both staff and visitors walking in the building's many corridors.

Dumas Beach, near Surat City in the state of Gujarat, is haunted by the sounds of strange cries and moaning noises which are most often heard by early morning visitors. The ghosts are thought to be the unquiet spirits of ritual cremations which have taken place here in the past.

☙ ☙ ☙

The countryside around Grenaby on the south side of the Isle of Man is haunted by the stone-throwing ghost of Jimmy Squarefoot, who appears with the head of a boar and two tusks on each side of his face. According to folklore, Jimmy was once an enormous pig who was carried around by a giant. He later transformed himself into a man and married a mortal woman, but the union didn't last due to his constant habit of throwing rocks and stones at his spouse. Eventually Jimmy was cast out and, unable to fully transform himself back into his original form, became doomed to walk the island, half-man, half-pig, forever.

On the night before the Japanese attack on Pearl Harbor – 7 December 1941 – two phantom armies were reported to have appeared in separate locations across Hawaii. Around the valley of Malu Honua on the southern side of the island, villagers reported hearing the sound of tramping feet as though a vast company of soldiers were passing down the valley and out towards the sea. On the western island of Kauai, another ghostly army was also said to have appeared, moving along the Lumahai Valley. On this occasion, the ghostly warriors were allegedly seen as well as heard.

ORIENTAL GHOSTS AND HAUNTINGS

The popularity of Hideo Nakata's 1998 horror film, *The Ring* (and an American remake directed by Gore Verbinski in 2002) has made Japanese ghosts more familiar to Western audiences in recent years. The novel by Koji Suzuki on which Nakata's film is based is itself based on the folklore ghost story of 'Banchō Sarayashiki', also known as the story 'Okiku and the Nine Plates'. The plot concerns a beautiful servant girl, who has been tricked by a spurned suitor into believing she has lost one of her employer's ten precious family plates, in order that she can be blackmailed into becoming his lover. However, she is murdered when she is thrown into a well after refusing his advances. Her ghost returns to count out loud the remaining nine plates, while the missing tenth plate is represented by a blood-curdling scream. Japanese apparitions are traditionally represented as figures dressed in white flowing robes with long black hair which hangs down, obscuring their faces. Okiku's ghost is said to haunt the well at Himeji Castle, a hilltop fortress and popular tourist destination in Hyōgo Prefecture in the Kansai region of Honshu Island.

One of Japan's most haunted locations is Aokigahara or The Sea of Trees, a forest at the base of Mount Fuji, a well-known suicide spot. Here, local people claim to have encountered the wandering apparitions of the many unfortunates who have taken their own lives, the faces of whom are also said to appear in the bark on the branches and trunks of the trees.

A ghostly Samurai warrior haunts the Gridley Tunnel, part of the old Yokosuka Naval Base on Honshu Island. Over the years, motorists driving down the narrow one-way road through the hillside have reported seeing an armoured figure standing in their way, as well as rather unnervingly appearing inside their vehicles, sitting in the back seats. Tradition states that the ghost is that of a warrior ambushed and hacked to death while attempting to avenge the death of his master.

The Weekly Mansion apartment block in Akasaka, Tokyo, is known for reports of white-clad spectral figures and the sensation of owners and visitors having their hair stroked by an unseen person as they lie in their beds at night.

Many ghost hunters have attempted to find Japan's most haunted house, the legendary Himuro Mansion, which is alleged to lie in a remote district on the outskirts of Tokyo. Here a family are said to have been slaughtered, leaving bloody handprints on the walls, and strange rituals involving the murder of a sacrificial maiden torn apart by a team of oxen or horses have resulted in stories of apparitions haunting the crumbling building in the woods. The story has become better known in the West following its inclusion as part of the horror video game series, *Fatal Frame* (2001–08).

Ghosts and the belief in the survival of the spirits of deceased relatives and ancestors form an important part of Chinese as well as Japanese culture. The Ghost Festival is a traditional Chinese holiday celebrated on the fourteenth or fifteenth day of the seventh month of the lunar year, itself known as the Ghost Month, which has its origins in both traditional Chinese folklore and Buddism. Gifts of food and clothing are prepared to pay respect to the spirits of deceased relatives, as well as to appease itinerant or wandering ghosts to prevent them entering houses and creating unwanted hauntings.

Many of China's historical buildings have paranormal associations. The Imperial Palace, known as 'The Forbidden City', home to the country's ruling emperors for over five centuries and today a national museum, is said to be haunted by mysterious animal shapes and the white-robed figure of a crying woman. Another female ghost has been seen at the Songpo Library in the Xicheng district of Beijing, said to be a courtesan to General Wu Sangui who committed suicide, while the abandoned British-built Chaonei church in Chaoyang, also in Beijing, is haunted by unearthly screams. The Wukang Mansion, a 1920s apartment building in Shanghai, has been plagued by the sound of disembodied footsteps and voices, and there are many other similar haunted buildings across the country.

☙ ☙ ☙

One afternoon in October 1997, two twelve-year-old schoolboys were walking home from a fishing outing near the village of Silkstone Common just over 3 miles west of Barnsley in South Yorkshire. As they crossed an area of farmland they saw the figure of a young girl coming towards them and both were struck by her strange appearance: the girl, who appeared to be around eight or nine years old, was dressed in decidedly old-fashioned clothes and surrounded by what they later described as a white mist. As she passed close by, she turned and looked at them and then instantly vanished. Frightened by their experience, the two boys hurried home and told their parents what had happened. The ghost was later identified as Emily Whitely, a local child who lived close to the spot where the boys described having their encounter: she had been killed at the age of eleven in a shotgun accident in 1908. When Emily's niece, who heard about the incident following a report in a local newspaper, showed the schoolboys a photograph of the dead child, they both confirmed that she was the person they had seen walking beside them.

13

SOME FAMOUS GHOST HUNTERS

The opening decade of the twenty-first century has seen ghost hunting and paranormal investigation become an increasing popular occupation across Britain. In 2005, it was calculated that 1,200 paranormal societies were active throughout the country, involving in the region of 5,000 amateur researchers and investigators. Some the very first British ghost hunters were Victorian scientists actually intent on debunking stories of ghosts and the paranormal. The esteemed Michael Faraday (1791–1867), regarded as 'one of the greatest scientific discoverers of all time', investigated table-tipping, a social phenomenon that came to England in the early 1850s following the spread of Spiritualism from America. Faraday was convinced that rather than spirits turning the tables, the movements were the result of unconscious muscle movement independent of the deliberate thoughts of the sitters. Another distinguished Victorian scientist, the chemist Sir William Crookes (1832–1919) who invented the cathode ray tube and discovered the element thallium, became fascinated with mediumistic phenomena and carried out personal investigations of some of the most famous mediums of the day including Daniel Dunglas Home, Florence Cook and Anna Eva Fay. Crookes was convinced that an alleged spirit personality known as 'Katie King', who materialised at many of the sittings he held in his house in London, was a genuine ghost in solid form.

During the course of the twentieth century, a number of individuals took an intense interest in paranormal matters and today, through their research and writings, are considered pioneering figures in the movement. The Australian Richard Hodgson (1855–1905) was the first professional full-time salaried ghost hunter who held official positions with the London Society for Psychical Research and the American Society for Psychical Research. Hodgson investigated the famous occultist Helena Blavatsky in India as well as the Neapolitan physical medium, Eusapia Palladino. However, it was an Englishman who is most identified as the first true ghost hunter.

Described as the 'father of modern ghost hunting', the Englishman Harry Price, conjuror, author, showman and psychical researcher extraordinaire, remains one of the most influential and inspiring figures in the history of paranormal investigation. Born in Holborn, London in 1881, Price became interested in a number of pursuits as a young man, including amateur dramatics, coin collecting and magic tricks. Having attended spiritualist séances both before and after the First World War, Price joined the London Society for Psychical Research in 1920, intent on becoming one of the leading paranormal researchers of the day. In 1925, he established his own organisation, the National Laboratory of Psychical Research, which for several years operated out of premises in Queensberry Place, South Kensington. Well versed in fraudulent séance room tricks, Price investigated many well-known mediums, including the Austrian Schneider brothers Willi and Rudi, the materialising mediums Helen Duncan (a Scotswoman) and Polishman Jan Guzyk, as well as Anna Rasmussen, the Danish 'Daylight Medium', so named for her ability to move objects without touching them or the need for darkened or blackout conditions. Unfortunately for Price, his ego was even greater than his psychical knowledge and he made many enemies during the course of his paranormal career, both within the Spiritualist community whose frauds he exposed, as well as among his ghost-hunting colleagues with whom he found difficult to co-operate and who treated his fondness for self-publicity with suspicion.

Price's continued love of the limelight brought him in contact with the popular press on many occasions and he was quickly identified in the public eye as one of the country's leading investigators. Several headline-grabbing adventures which took place during the 1920s and 1930s included the Brocken Experiment, which involved an attempt to transform a live goat into a human being with the aid of a magical formula; the case of Gef, the Talking Mongoose who lived in a remote farmhouse on the Isle of Man and was known to ride around the island on a bus as well as singing hymns and reciting poetry; and the opening of the famous locked box of the eighteenth-century prophetess, Joanna Southcott. Price chronicled his investigations in a number of books which are still very readable today; signed first editions of which continue to be sought after by collectors and enthusiasts.

They include *Leaves From a Psychist's Case-Book* (1933), *Confessions of a Ghost-Hunter* (1936), *Fifty Years of Psychical Research* (1939) and an autobiography, *Search for Truth* (1942). Although his investigation of Borley Rectory remains his most famous case, this has tended to overshadow other and potentially more convincing research, including the investigation of the Schneider brothers and the curious incident of 'Rosalie', an alleged spirit child which appeared during a closed physical séance in a house in London in 1937. Harry Price died at his home in Pulborough, West Sussex on 29 March 1948.

A contemporary of Harry Price, the Irishman Elliott O'Donnell, was described on occasion as 'the Champ' and 'the greatest ghost hunter of all time'. O'Donnell, who died in 1965 at the age of ninety-three, wrote several dozen books chronicling his supernatural adventures in his native Ireland, as well as in England and America, in which he claimed to have seen the face of a phantom in a mirror, interviewed a man who was shaved by a ghostly barber and witnessed the apparition of a skeleton looking in through a window, as well as an account of staying in a spectral hotel that had disappeared when he went back to collect his bags. Although he never claimed to have ridden on the ghost train that he discovered was said to drive at express speed through an American railway station, O'Donnell was adamant that he had had his first paranormal experience at the age of five when a strange tall figure with yellow eyes, 'long arms, and a head too big for its body' drifted through his bedroom in the family home in County Clare.

The release of the 2013 paranormal-themed horror film *The Conjuring*, directed by James Wan, was instrumental in bringing the career of American husband and wife ghost hunters Ed and Lorraine Warren to a wider audience. In the early 1950s, the Warrens founded the New England Society for Psychic Research with the intention of investigating haunted buildings in the New England area. Lorraine (b. 1927), a trance medium

and clairvoyant and Edward (1926–2006), who later broadened
his paranormal palate to include the identification and exorcism
of demons and similar possessing 'entities', brought their own
distinctive style to the research of American hauntings and
claimed to have examined over 10,000 cases in a joint career
spanning five decades. A feature of many of the Warrens'

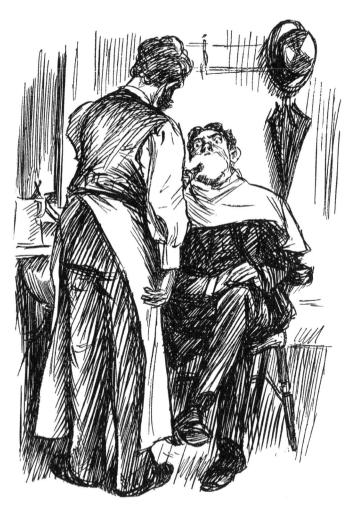

investigations was to collect a physical item of some aspect of the case under investigation as a souvenir, the resulting collection being known today as The Warrens' Occult Museum, located in the family home in Monroe, Connecticut. Like Harry Price, the Warrens' most famous case is an allegedly most haunted house, in this instance at the centre of the well-known Amityville Horror, while their other prominent investigations include the 1971 Perron family (the subject of *The Conjuring*) whose Rhode Island home was said to be haunted by an early nineteenth-century witch; the 1981 Arne Johnson 'Demon Murder' case; the 1983 Bill Ramsey 'Werewolf Exorcism'; and the Smurl family, who claimed to share their Pennsylvania home with a demon in 1986. The Warrens authored a number of books on their many investigations and were the subject of *The Demonologist*, a biography written by Gerald Brittle, published in 1980.

Another professional researcher who spent much time investigating American hauntings was Viennese-born Hans Holzer (1920–2009), a prolific author on paranormal subjects whose writings encompassed haunted houses, ESP, witchcraft and UFOs as well as astrology, demonic possession and, most importantly, survival after death, in which he came to be a firm believer. Holzer, whose other interests included history and archaeology, felt that discarnate spirits were at the root of many reported hauntings and ghost sightings and often carried out investigations accompanied by spiritualist mediums including Ethel Johnson Meyers and witch, astrologer and sensitive, Sybil Leek. His researches brought him to the conclusion that there are essentially three types of ghost: the stone tape imprint that we have seen earlier; 'true ghosts', the spirits of persons who have met particularly violent or tragic deaths who are unable to move on and so find themselves in limbo in the psychic fabric of our world; and 'stay-behinds', strong-willed ghosts who are unwilling to leave places or physical locations which meant much to them in life. Like the Warrens, Holzer felt compelled to investigate the

Amityville case and came to the (incorrect) conclusion that the house in Ocean Drive had been built on a former Shinnecock Indian burial ground, a theme that was later developed to great effect by director Tobe Hooper in his 1982 film, *Poltergeist*. Holzer toured Britain on a number of occasions and was invited to address the Ghost Club. He published a photograph taken in Winchester Cathedral which appeared to show the hooded figures of ghostly monks and felt he had also photographed ghosts in the haunted trailer home of go-go dancer Rita Atlanta, as well as in a house on Ardmore Boulevard, Los Angeles. For several years, the ghost hunter was married to Catherine Buxhoeveden, a sixth-generation descendant of Catherine the Great of Russia.

The eminent Scottish astronomer Archie Roy (1924–2012), known as the 'Glasgow Ghostbuster', was a prominent member of both the London Society for Psychical Research and the Scottish Society for Psychical Research who, like Sir William Crookes, felt it was a scientist's duty to investigate and try to find answers for unexplained phenomena such as mediumship and hauntings. His interest in psychical research began after stumbling across several books on ghosts and spiritualism in the library at Glasgow University, in which he was surprised to find that respected academics and scientists such as Crookes, Sir Oliver Lodge and William James had also felt it necessary to make an examination of the supernatural. Roy investigated a Glaswegian poltergeist haunting in Northgate Quadrant, Balornock, and was also a member of PRISM (Psychical Research Involving Selected Mediums), a specialist group within the London Society for Psychical Research that made an active study of psychics and mediumship, investigating the claims of twenty-seven mediums over a five-year period. Roy wrote several novels and three books on psychical research. He was also a consultant and featured commentator on the 1996 *Ghosthunters* television series hosted by former *Tomorrow's World* presenter William Woollard.

Born in Letchworth Garden City in 1923, Peter Underwood has enjoyed a unique seven-decade paranormal career that has justly earned him the title 'King of Ghost Hunters'. Having maternal grandparents who lived at a haunted Hertfordshire mill, Underwood became interested in ghosts at an early age. In 1947, he corresponded with Harry Price and spent a night in the ruins of Borley Rectory. At Price's invitation he joined the Ghost Club and was the recipient of one of the great ghost hunter's final letters shortly before his sudden death. Following a successful career with London publisher J.M. Dent & Sons, Underwood's first book, *A Gazetteer of British Ghosts*, was published in 1971, after which he went solo and became a full-time writer, issuing a string of paranormal titles as well as scripting and presenting radio and television broadcasts on ghosts and hauntings including the BBC's highly regarded *The Ghost Hunters* from 1975, which also featured contributions from Andrew Green, Benson Herbert and Geoffrey Croom-Hollingsworth. With over fifty titles on subjects including haunted houses, occultism, exorcism and ghost hunting, Underwood's books have proved inspirational to several generations of modern writers and researchers.

Modern twenty-first century paranormal-themed reality television programmes in both Britain and America have brought ghost hunting and psychical investigation to a wide audience, fuelling interest and controversy in equal measure. *Most Haunted*, which first aired in May 2002 and survived fourteen series over eight years, including several sensational live specials and spin-off programmes, visited many haunted locations around the country and brought several psychics and researchers into the public eye, including mediums Derek Acorah (b. 1950) and David Wells (b. 1960), as well as ghost hunter Phil Whyman (b. 1971), parapsychologist Dr Ciarán O'Keeffe (b. 1971) and paranormal historian Richard Felix (b. 1949). In America, two former plumbers, Jason Hawes (b. 1971) and Grant Wilson (b. 1974), founders of The Atlantic Paranormal Society (TAPS), have become semi-professional paranormal researchers thanks to the popularity of their syndicated reality investigation programme *Ghost Hunters*, which was first broadcast on the Sci-Fi Channel (now known as SyFy) in October 2004.

14

GHOST SOCIETIES AND PARANORMAL ORGANISATIONS

The following societies and organisations have been closely linked with the serious study of ghosts and similar paranormal phenomena for the past 150 years. Today all have active programmes for members and much of their research material and archives is available online.

THE GHOST CLUB

Founded in Cambridge in 1851, the Ghost Club is the oldest organisation in the world dedicated to the study of ghosts and the paranormal. Originally named the Ghost Society, it was created by Revd B.F. Westcott, later Bishop of Durham, and members at the time included future prime minister, Arthur Balfour, and the soon-to-be Archbishop of Canterbury, Edward Benson. Around 1862, the Ghost Society was succeeded by the London Ghost Club, whose ranks included, amongst a smattering of original members, the Registrar of Cambridge University, the Hon. A.H. Gordon. This second incarnation was only active for a few years during the 1860s and little is known about its activities or meetings.

In 1882, the Ghost Club was revived and became an established private society whose invited members convened over dinner to listen to lectures on psychical and paranormal subjects. Members during this period, which lasted for over fifty years up until the mid-1930s, included writer Sir Arthur Conan Doyle, physicist Sir William Crookes, Sir Oliver Lodge, the pioneer of radio, the poet W.B. Yeats, newspaper editor W.T. Stead, Admiral W. Usborne Moore, and ghost hunter Harry Price. Members addressed each other as 'Brother Ghost' and the club was an all-male preserve until 1926, after which an Annual Ladies Guest Night was established and one token female member was elected. By 1936, however, membership had dwindled and the Ghost Club was wound up.

In 1938, a second revival took place, instigated by Harry Price who acted as chairman. Again, membership was by invitation only and limited to 500 people. This time, women were admitted as members and the club met every six weeks: the 500th meeting (calculated from the start of the first revival in 1882) was held at the Savoy Hotel in London on 9 April 1947. Members from this period included the poet Siegfried Sassoon, author Algernon Blackwood, Sir Osbert Sitwell, criminal psychologist Dr Donald West, Sir Ernest Jelf, spiritualist Bernard Abdy Collins, and society ear piercer Cyril Wilkinson. Following Harry Price's death in 1948, the Ghost Club was again disbanded.

A third revival took place in 1954, headed by a council comprising Percival Seward, a businessman; Leonard Kingston, a former RAF Pathfinder pilot; Dr Christabel Nicholson, Cyril Wilkinson, and Peter Underwood. In 1960, Underwood was elected as Ghost Club president and went on to serve in that capacity for over thirty years. The club organised regular lectures and trips to haunted houses and other locations around the country and invited members from this period included writer and broadcaster Michael Bentine, actor Peter Cushing, thriller writer Dennis Wheatley, medium Ena Twigg, Lord Dowding, explorer Colonel John Blashford-Snell, Dan Farson (great-nephew of Bram Stoker), and actor Peter Sellers.

In 1993, Peter Underwood resigned as president and went on to establish his own Ghost Club Society. The Ghost Club continued as an open-subscription organisation, headed at first by researcher Tom Perrott and later between 1998 and 2005 by barrister Alan Murdie. He was succeeded by Kathy Gearing, only to return to the post in 2009. The Ghost Club continues to organise on-site vigils and investigations and issues a regular journal. Among the many haunted locations previously visited include Battle Abbey, Glasgow's Museum of Transport, RAF Montrose Air Museum, Michelham Priory and Coalhouse Fort.

Website: www.ghostclub.org.uk

SOCIETY FOR PSYCHICAL RESEARCH (SPR)

In early December 1869, two Cambridge intellectuals, Henry Sidgwick and Frederick W.H. Myers, took an evening walk under the stars. At some point their conversation turned to the possibility of carrying out serious and controlled research into the then taboo subjects of spiritualism, hauntings, prophetic dreams and similar unexplained phenomena that the two men were both interested in and eager to understand. It would be thirteen years before the seeds of their discussion eventually bore fruit, with the founding of the Society for Psychical Research (also known variously as the London SPR and the Incorporated SPR) in London in February 1882. At that time, the impetus was provided by Edmund Dawson Rogers, a convinced spiritualist, and William Barrett, Professor of Physics at the Royal College of Science in Dublin. It was Henry Sidgwick, though, who became the SPR's first president and the society adopted as its mission statement the study of 'those faculties of man, real or supposed, which appear to be inexplicable on any generally recognised hypothesis'.

In its early years, much of the SPR's work was carried out by a small council of members which comprised Frederick Myers; the psychologist Edmund Gurney; Eleanor Sidgwick, Henry Sidgwick's wife and the principal of Newnham College, Cambridge; Richard Hodgson, the world's first professional psychical researcher; and Frank Podmore, a civil servant and founding member of the Fabian Society. Other distinguished early members included former Ghost Clubber Sir William Crookes, Lord Rayleigh (John William Strutt, 3rd Baron), the Nobel Prize-winning discoverer of argon, Sir Oliver Lodge, and the naturalist Alfred Russell Wallace.

The society established several committees to examine specific paranormal phenomena and its associated effects. These included the physical phenomena of Spiritualism, principally materialisations and similar man-made ghosts associated with the séance room; haunted houses and other buildings; telepathy and thought-transference; Mesmerism; and human auras and similar phenomena (known at the time as the 'odyle' or 'odic force'). There was also a literary committee involved in publishing research papers and the establishment of a reference library. The society's main publication, beginning in October 1882, was the multi-volume *Proceedings*, which was followed in 1884 by a regular journal. Four years after its founding, the SPR issued its first major work, a two-volume study of telepathy and the phenomenon of crisis ghosts titled *Phantasms of the Living*. Research for the study had involved an extensive data-gathering exercise termed the 'Census of Hallucinations', which involved submitting a questionnaire to just over 15,000 people, 10 per cent of whom reported experiencing some kind of supernormal phenomena in which they obtained information by an unnatural process, either through a dream or the witnessing of some kind of apparition.

During the course of its 130-plus year history, the SPR has had many notable personages serving as president, including anthropologist Andrew Lang, zoologist Sir Alister Hardy, psychologist John Beloff and astronomer Bernard Carr. The society holds regular lectures and study days for members and publishes papers and articles through its journal and *Paranormal Review* newsletter.

Website: www.spr.ac.uk

AMERICAN SOCIETY FOR PSYCHICAL RESEARCH (ASPR)

Stimulated by a visit to the country by SPR founder William Barrett, the American Society for Psychical Research was founded soon after by a group of Boston intellectuals which included philosopher William James. In its early years, the society was affiliated to the London SPR for financial reasons and carried out similar research, but in 1906 it achieved independence. In 1925, internal politics concerning the investigation of controversial physical medium Mina Crandon caused several members who were unhappy with the ASPR's continued devotion to Spiritualism to break away and form a rival organisation, the Boston SPR, which survived as a smaller, separate society until 1941, when the two groups were reunited. Like the British SPR, its American counterpart publishes a regular newsletter and journal and has a research library of over 10,000 books devoted to paranormal subjects.

Website: www.aspr.com

ASSOCIATION FOR THE SCIENTIFIC STUDY OF ANOMALOUS PHENOMENA (ASSAP)

The scientific investigation of ghosts and hauntings as well as UFOs, Extrasensory Perception (ESP), coincidences, paranormal photographs and similar Fortean phenomena is the primary goal of ASSAP, founded in 1981 by a collective of similar-minded researchers including photographic expert Vernon Harrison, pictorial researcher and author Hilary Evans and ufologist Jenny Randles; its first president was former Goon and author, Michael Bentine, who had a long interest in the paranormal. The society runs an accredited training course for investigators and is affiliated with several regional paranormal groups across the UK.

Website: www.assap.ac.uk

CHURCHES' FELLOWSHIP FOR PSYCHICAL AND SPIRITUAL STUDIES

Formed originally in 1953 as the Churches' Fellowship for Psychic Study, the Fellowship exists to promote the study of psychical and religious experiences within a basic Christian concept. In order to do this, it organises lectures and study groups and produces two regular publications, the *Christian Parapsychologist* and the *Quarterly Review*.

Website: www.churchesfellowship.co.uk

UNITARIAN SOCIETY FOR PSYCHICAL STUDIES

Established in 1965 by Revd G. Stanley Whitby and his wife, Revd Florence Whitby, the society promotes the critical and open-minded study of all aspects of psychical phenomena, including ghosts and hauntings. It organises regular meetings and publishes the *Psychical Studies* journal.

Website: www.ukunitarians.org.uk/psychical/

BIBLIOGRAPHY AND FURTHER READING

Many published ghost books have established themselves as classic titles and more works are being issued every year. The following is a list of 100 paranormal books and guides that no self-respecting ghost hunter should be without:

Abbott, Geoffrey, *Ghosts of the Tower of London* (Heinemann: London, 1980)

Adams, Paul, Brazil, Eddie and Underwood, Peter, *The Borley Rectory Companion* (The History Press: Stroud, 2009)

——, *Shadows in the Nave: A Guide to the Haunted Churches of England* (The History Press: Stroud, 2011)

Alexander, Marc, *Haunted Churches & Abbeys of Britain* (Arthur Barker: London, 1978)

——, *Haunted Houses You May Visit* (Sphere Books Ltd: London, 1982)

——, *Haunted Inns* (Frederick Muller Ltd: London, 1973)

Anson, Jay, *The Amityville Horror* (Prentice Hall: New York, 1977)

Arnold, Neil, *Paranormal London* (The History Press: London, 2011)

Baldwin, Gay, *Ghosts of Knighton Gorges* (Gay Baldwin: Cowes, 2010)

——, *The Original Ghosts of the Isle of Wight* (Gay Baldwin: Cowes, 1997)

Bander, Peter, *Carry on Talking: How Dead are the Voices?* (Colin Smythe: Gerrards Cross, 1972)

Bardens, Dennis, *Ghosts & Hauntings* (The Zeus Press: London, 1965)

Beloff, John, *Parapsychology: A Concise History* (The Athlone Press: London, 1993)

Bennett, Sir Ernest, *Haunted Houses: A Survey of the Evidence* (Faber & Faber: London, 1939)

Berger, Arthur & Joyce, *The Encyclopedia of Parapsychology & Psychical Research* (Paragon House: New York, 1991)

Brandon, David and Brooke, Alan, *Haunted London Underground* (The History Press: Stroud, 2009)

Brazil, Eddie, *Haunted High Wycombe* (The History Press: Stroud, 2013)

Broughall, Tony and Adams, Paul, *Two Haunted Counties: A Ghost Hunter's Companion to Bedfordshire & Hertfordshire* (The Limbury Press: Luton, 2010)

Brown, Theo, *Devon Ghosts* (Jarrold: Norwich, 1982)

Brown, Raymond Lamont, *Phantoms of the Theatre* (Thomas Nelson: London, 1977)

Clarke, Roger, *A Natural History of Ghosts: 500 Years of Hunting for Proof* (Penguin Books: London, 2012)

Cornell, Tony, *Investigating the Paranormal* (Helix Press: New York, 2002)

Crowe, Catherine, *The Night Side of Nature* (T.C. Newby: London, 1848)

Dingwall, Eric J., Goldney, Kathleen M. and Hall, Trevor H., *The Haunting of Borley Rectory* (Duckworth: London, 1956)

Edmunds, Simeon, *Spiritualism: A Critical Survey* (Aquarian Press: London, 1966)

Eyre, Kathleen, *Lancashire Ghosts* (Dalesman Books: Clapham, 1974)

Farquharson-Coe, A., *Devon's Ghosts* (James Pike Ltd: St Ives, 1975)

Farrant, David, *Dark Journey* (British Psychic & Occult Society: London, 2004)

Farson, Daniel, *The Hamlyn Book of Ghosts in Fact & Fiction* (Hamlyn: London, 1978)

Fielding, Yvette and O'Keeffe, Ciarán, *Ghost Hunters: A Guide to Investigating the Paranormal* (Hodder & Stoughton: London, 2006)

Fontana, David, *Is There an Afterlife?* (O Books: London, 2005)

Forman, Joan, *The Haunted South* (Jarrold Publishing: Norwich, 1989)

Foy, Robin, *Witnessing the Impossible* (Torcal Publications: Diss, 2008)

Fraser, John, *Ghost Hunting: A Survivor's Guide* (The History Press: Stroud, 2010)

Fuller, John G., *The Ghost of Flight 401* (Souvenir Press: London, 1976)

Gauld, Alan, *Mediumship & Survival* (Paladin Books: London, 1983)

Gauld, Alan and Cornell, A.D., *Poltergeists* (Routledge & Kegan Paul: London, 1979)

Goss, Michael, *The Evidence for Phantom Hitchhikers* (The Aquarian Press: Wellingborough, 1984)

Green, Andrew, *Ghosts of the South East* (David & Charles: Newton Abbot, 1976)

——, *Our Haunted Kingdom* (Wolfe Publishing Ltd: London, 1973)

Guiley, Rosemary Ellen, *The Encyclopedia of Ghosts & Spirits* (Checkmark Books: New York, 1992)

Haining, Peter, *Ghosts: The Illustrated History* (Sidgwick & Jackson: London, 1979)

——, *The Mammoth Book of True Hauntings* (Constable & Robinson Ltd: London, 2008)

Hall, Trevor H., *New Light on Old Ghosts* (Duckworth: London, 1965)

Hallam, Jack, *The Ghosts' Who's Who* (David & Charles: Newton Abbot, 1977)

Hallowell, Michael J. and Ritson, Darren W., *The South Shields Poltergeist* (The History Press: Stroud, 2009)

——, *The Haunting of Willington Mill* (The History Press: Stroud, 2011)

Harper, Charles G., *Haunted Houses* (Chapman & Hall Ltd: London, 1907)

Harries, John, *The Ghost Hunter's Road Book* (Frederick Muller Ltd: London, 1968)

Hippisley Coxe, Antony D., *Haunted Britain* (Hutchinson & Co.: London, 1973)

Holder, Geoff, *Poltergeist Over Scotland* (The History Press: Stroud, 2013)

Holzer, Hans, *The Great British Ghost Hunt* (Bobbs-Merrill: Indianapolis, 1975)

Hopkins, R. Thurston, *Adventures with Phantoms* (Quality Press: London, 1946)

Jones, Richard, *Haunted London* (New Holland Publishers: London, 2011)

King, William H., *Haunted Bedfordshire: A Ghostly Compendium* (The Book Castle: Dunstable, 2005)

Lindley, Charles, *Lord Halifax's Ghost Book* (Geoffrey Bles Ltd: London, 1936)

MacKenzie, Andrew, *Hauntings and Apparitions* (Heinemann: London, 1982)

Maple, Eric, *The Realm of Ghosts* (Robert Hale: London, 1964)

Markham, Len, *Ten Yorkshire Mysteries* (Countryside Books: Newbury, 1995)

Matthews, Rupert, *Haunted Surrey* (The History Press: Stroud, 2011)

McEwan, Graham J., *Haunted Churches of England* (Robert Hale: London, 1989)

Moss, Peter, *Ghosts Over Britain* (Elm Tree Books: London, 1977)

Newton, Toyne, *The Demonic Connection* (Blandford Press: Poole, 1987)

O'Donnell, Elliott, *Haunted Britain* (Rider & Co.: London, 1948)

——, *Phantoms of the Night* (Rider & Co.: London, 1956)

Owen, A.R.G. and Simms, Victor, *Science & the Spook* (Dennis Dobson: London, 1971)

Playfair, Guy Lyon, *This House is Haunted* (Souvenir Press: London, 1980)

Price, Harry, *Fifty Years of Psychical Research* (Longmans: London, 1939)

——, *The End of Borley Rectory* (Harrap: London, 1946)

——, *The Most Haunted House in England* (Longmans: London, 1940)

——, *Poltergeist Over England* (Country Life: London, 1945)

Randles, Jenny, *Paranormal Source Book* (BCA: London, 1999)

Raudive, Konstantin, *Breakthrough: An Amazing Experiment in Electronic Communication with the Dead* (Colin Smyth: Gerrards Cross, 1971)

Ritson, Darren W., *Haunted Carlisle* (The History Press: Stroud, 2012)

——, *Supernatural North: True Ghost Stories* (Amberley Publishing: Stroud, 2009)

Rogo, D. Scott, *The Haunted House Handbook* (Tempo Books: New York, 1978)

Rogo, D. Scott and Bayless, Raymond, *Phone Calls from the Dead* (Prentice Hall: New York, 1979)

Ronson, Mark, *Haunted Castles* (Hamlyn: London, 1982)

Screeton, Paul, *Quest for the Hexham Heads* (CFZ Press: Bideford, 2012)

Sitwell, Sacheverell, *Poltergeists* (Faber & Faber: London, 1940)

Spencer, John and Wells, Tony, *Ghost Watching: The Ghosthunter's Handbook* (Virgin Books: London, 1994)

Stemman, Roy, *Spirit Communication* (Piatkus Books Ltd: London, 2005)

Tabori, Paul, *Harry Price: The Biography of a Ghost-hunter* (Athenaeum Press: London, 1950)

——, *Pioneers of the Unseen* (Souvenir Press: London, 1972)

Taylor, Troy, *Season of the Witch: The Haunted History of the Bell Witch of Tennessee* (Whitechapel Productions: Alton, 1999)

Thurston, Herbert, *Ghosts and Poltergeists* (Burns Oates: London, 1953)

Tyrrell, G.N.M., *Apparitions* (Duckworth: London, 1953)

Underwood, Peter, *A Gazetteer of British Ghosts* (Souvenir Press: London, 1971)

——, *Ghosts & How to See Them* (Brockhampton Press: London, 1993)

——, *Haunted London* (Harrap: London, 1973)

——, *Irish Ghosts: A Ghost Hunter's Guide* (Amberley Publishing: Stroud, 2012)

——, *No Common Task: The Autobiography of a Ghost-hunter* (Harrap: London, 1983)

——, *The Ghost Club – A History* (The Limbury Press: Luton, 2010)

——, *The Ghost Hunter's Guide* (Blandford Press: Poole, 1986)

——, *This Haunted Isle* (Harrap: London, 1984)

——, *Where the Ghosts Walk* (Souvenir Press: London, 2013)

Whyman, Phil, *Phil Whyman's Dead Haunted: Paranormal Encounters & Investigations* (New Holland Publishers Ltd.: London, 2007)

Wilson, Colin, *Afterlife* (Harrap: London, 1985)

——, *Poltergeist!: A Study in Destructive Haunting* (New English Library: London, 1981)

——, *The Occult* (Mayflower: St Albans, 1973)

SOME PARANORMAL WEBSITES

As well as the websites mentioned in other parts of this book, the following Internet sites contain useful information on ghosts, hauntings and similar supernormal phenomena:

www.mysteriousbritain.co.uk
Mysterious Britain & Ireland: A comprehensive resource of information on the hauntings, legends, folklore and mysterious places of the British Isles.

www.paranormaldatabase.com
The Paranormal Database: A comprehensive and continually updated online gazetteer of ghosts and hauntings across England, Scotland, Ireland, Wales and the Channel Islands.

www.harrypricewebsite.co.uk
The Harry Price website: An online collection of articles on the career of Britain's famous ghost hunter, including a comprehensive section on the Borley Rectory case.

www.davidfarrant.org
David Farrant, Psychic Investigator: Known for his involvement in the Highgate Vampire affair of the late 1960s/early 1970s and founder of the long-standing British Psychic and Occult Society, David Farrant (b. 1946) has carried out personal investigations of many haunted buildings and locations around Britain, details of which – as well as information on his many books and video documentaries – are available on this website.

www.peterunderwood.org.uk
Peter Underwood: The renowned ghost hunter's official website, which includes biographical information, photographs and a bibliography.

www.ghostresearch.org
Ghost Research Society: The GRS, originally known as The Ghost Trackers Club, was founded in 1977 to collect real-life reports of ghosts, poltergeists, hauntings and survival-after-death experiences across America. The society president is Dale Kaczmarek (b.1952), one of America's most experienced ghost hunters.

www.prairieghosts.com
American Hauntings: Website of author and ghost hunter Troy Taylor (b. 1966), founder of the American Ghost Society, which contains links to The Haunted Museum online resource on the history of paranormal and psychical research.

ABOUT
THE AUTHOR

PAUL ADAMS was born in Epsom, Surrey in 1966. Brought up on a diet of Hammer films and British pulp-horror literature, a major preoccupation with the paranormal began in the mid-1970s. Employed as a draughtsman in the UK construction industry for over thirty years, he has worked in three haunted buildings but has yet to see a true ghost. As well as the history of psychical research, his main interests at present are in materialisation mediumship and the physical phenomena of Spiritualism. He has contributed articles to several specialist paranormal periodicals and acted as editor and publisher for *Two Haunted Counties* (2010), the memoirs of Luton ghost hunter Tony Broughall. Adams is the co-author of *The Borley Rectory Companion* (2009), *Shadows in the Nave* (2011) and *Extreme Hauntings* (2013), and has written *Haunted Luton and Dunstable* (2012), *Haunted St Albans* (2013), *Ghosts & Gallows* (2012), and *Written in Blood* (2014), a history of vampires and vampirism in British culture. He is also an amateur mycologist and viola-player and has lived in Luton since 2006.

Website: www.pauladamsauthor.co.uk
Twitter: @PaulAdamsAuthor